Atomic Words

ATOMIC WORDS

CUT THROUGH THE NOISE AND
DELIVER IMPACTFUL COMMUNICATION

GABE ARNOLD
CEO OF BUSINESS MARKETING ENGINE

ISBN: 978-1-95-315367-8

Published by

If you are interested in publishing through Lifestyle Entrepreneurs Press, write to: *Publishing@LifestyleEntrepreneursPress.com*

Publications or foreign rights acquisition of our catalog books. Learn More: *www.LifestyleEntrepreneursPress.com*

Printed in the USA

Advance Praise

I was so excited when I heard that my friend Gabe Arnold was writing a book.

Watching the evolution of his regular emails over the past few years—which began as updates about his business but quickly morphed into compelling stories with profound lessons for his readers—it was obvious that a book was in his future.

And now it's here.

With *Atomic Words: Cut Through the Noise and Deliver Impactful Communication*, Gabe practices what he preaches...while writing in a friendly style that, in his words, is like having a cup of coffee with a friend...with lesson after lesson, some hiding in plain sight...and some painfully obvious.

I guarantee you will be a better person after reading this book.

His writing style is a calming teaching style with examples throughout...with an emphasis on impact.

Gabe lays out the tools in an organized way...tools that every entrepreneur or business leader can put to use to create consistent, congruent and courageous communication with their audience.

He makes a compelling case that writing is the one tool we all have in our toolbox that will never become obsolete…and the more we write, the more impact we make.

And that's whether we communicate through email, letters, a journal…and in the best case, a book…using "atomic words" that are all our own.

He delivers on the promise in the title by cutting through the noise from all other books on this topic… with an infectious writing style…using his own "atomic words" to set a good example for all of us.

— Brian Kurtz, Titans Marketing and author of *Overdeliver: Build a Business for a Lifetime Playing the Long Game in Direct Response Marketing* and *The Advertising Solution*.

Contents

Disclaimer & Warning

This book is designed to provide information, motivation, and entertainment to our readers. It is based on the author's personal opinions and experiences with the subject matter and is made available to the public with the understanding that neither the author nor the publisher are engaged to render any type of psychological, legal, accounting, medical, nutritional, or any other kind of professional advice.

The author and publisher are providing this book and its contents on an "as is" basis and make no representations, warranties, or guarantees of any kind, expressed or implied, with respect to this book or its contents. The author and publisher disclaim all such representations and warranties. In addition, while every effort was made to ensure that the information in this book was correct at press time, the author and publisher do not represent or warrant that the information accessible via this book is accurate, complete, or current.

Neither the publisher nor any authors, contributors, or other representatives shall be held liable or responsible to any person or entity with respect to any loss, injury, disruption, or damage, including but not limited to any physical, psychological, emotional, financial, commercial, or any other damages caused, or alleged to have been caused, directly or indirectly, by the use of this book or the information contained herein. This is a comprehensive limitation of liability that applies to all damages of any kind, including (without limitation) compensatory, direct, indirect, special, incidental or consequential damages; loss of income or profit; loss of or damage to property; and claims of third parties. No warranty may be created or extended by sales representatives or by any written or electronic sales materials used in the sale and distribution of this book.

Every person and every life situation is different, and the information contained in this book may not be suitable for all readers. Reading this book does not guarantee that all readers' experiences will be comparable to that of the author or of other readers. It is advised that all readers seek the services of a competent professional before beginning any legal course of action, lifestyle change, health practice, or other improvement program. Your use of this book signifies your acceptance of this disclaimer. Additionally, the names of some people have been changed in this book to protect their privacy. The stories in this book are based on real-life events but may be fictionalized at some level for the purpose of teaching the concepts in this book.

Additionally, the author would like to warn the reader that using any of the communication tools, frameworks, principles, and strategies contained in this for harm or for evil is not advisable. Using good tools for bad work will almost always result in more damage to yourself than to others. Please, please use the powerful information in this book to make the world a better place. That is what the book is intended to do, make your world and the world around you a more peaceful and loving place.

With Gratitude

This book is the culmination of over two decades of study and practice in the art of communication. Whether it is the spoken or the written word, our ability to communicate effectively has such a profound effect on our own lives and the lives of those around us.

Writing a book is a *massive* undertaking. I have written a few smaller, completely unnoteworthy books in the past, but this book is the first book that I've written that I am truly proud of. I've taken many clients through the book-writing process over the past few years. I love coaching clients on writing their books, and my team and I love ghost-writing books for our clients as well. This is because they often have the most magnificent ideas and solutions to share with the world.

We record our interviews with our clients and then simply write their words for them. And what is truly magical about writing a book is that when you're done, you've created something that can (and hopefully will) outlive you. A book is one way to actually leave a legacy for those who come after us, and I am immensely grateful to all the authors who have done that work for me over the years.

Even with all that experience of helping others write their books, I had no idea how much work it was going to be to write my own. This book would not have been possible without the love and support of my beautiful, patient, and ever-amazing partner Rachel Strong. We started our path together as business partners, and I'm incredibly grateful that in time we also chose each other to be life partners.

Rachel, you give me beauty, peace, and kindness every day. Your relentless study of me, and your endless service and support of me, is the reason why we have the life we have. It's also the reason why our team gets to have a fully present, grounded, and intentional CEO to lead them.

And even more importantly than all the life and business adventures that we've been able to embark on together, you are the most amazing and thoughtful mother to our son, Arlis. I know that your dedication to him will be one of the reasons that he looks back and says, "I had a wonderful childhood." Thank you for loving him and serving him with the same passion and intentionality that you show me.

And to my son, Arlis, the moment that you came into this world I knew you were going to be a bright shining star for our big, beautiful world. The day of your birth was one of the happiest and most transformational days of my life. You and I spent the first few hours of your life together while your mom was in surgery, and I told you about all of my dreams for our life together. Arlis, you have inspired me more than any other person to chase my dreams and to do the hard work that is required to truly understand myself and to truly understand what I believe and why.

This book is a result of me doing the deep work required to understand what effective and impactful communication is made of. Arlis, you are already an amazing and effective communicator and a voracious reader. You are strong and you are kind. You make me proud of you every single day, and I will never cease to thank the Universe for giving me the privilege and great honor to be your father.

To my siblings and their spouses: Heather and Jim, Amos and Katie, Caleb and Gina, Judah and Nikki, Cody and Kaya, and Andrew and Taylor: thank you for loving me and accepting me through all the ups and downs that I have gone through. I know I unintentionally dragged you into those ups and downs at times as well. So thank you for showing me grace. Thank you for backing the book. You have all been so incredibly generous, and it means the world to me. I am very grateful for the fact that you are all my siblings and some of my dearest friends. I'm proud of each of you and grateful for the opportunity that I was given to grow up with you and also have seasons where I have been able to guide and support you.

To my ever-growing list of nieces and nephews: I love each of you as if you were my own children. You all melt my heart and make me so proud to be your uncle. I will always be here for you, no matter what happens. Zeke, I want to give you a special shout out to say thank you for being so generous and donating to my book campaign as well. You are the oldest cousin, and I am the oldest boy in our sibling group. I know what that weight feels like and I am committed to supporting you in any way I can. Thank you for being patient with me and showing me grace when I haven't deserved it. I promise to keep working on myself and showing up for you and all of the cousins in better and better ways over the coming years.

To Pam Kesling: Your generosity and support mean the world to me. I am truly grateful that you are part of my life and that Arlis has you in his life as well. Thank you for being so kind.

To Christian and Danielle: I appreciate how you both continually choose to grow in your leadership abilities. Without your love and support I would never have been able to grow our company, Business Marketing Engine, the way we have.

To Doug Beaver: You are one of my oldest and dearest friends, mentors, and coaches. When it comes to effective communication, you have faithfully demonstrated to me how a true leader lives, acts, and communicates. I would never have been able to reach the levels of success that I have today without your friendship and guidance. You have stood in the gap for me so many times. Thanks for giving me my first paid music gig and thank you for taking me to the Odeon to see all those rock shows. You've been an amazing father figure in my life for so many years, and I am a better man because of it.

To Brian Kurtz: If it wasn't for your example, I would never have been able to become a writer like I am today. When I first realized (by your example) that it was possible to write about umpiring Little League games while, at the same time, teaching marketing lessons, I decided to become a copywriter. Your example has inspired me to write and has led me to make millions of dollars. More importantly though, your example of living a 100/0 life has helped me grow and mature as a leader, and my life is richer because of you. Thank you for being a living example of what a true overdelivering servant leader is.

To my friend Jay Crouch: I hope when you open this book up and see your name here that you understand at a deep level how impactful you have been in my life. This book would have never happened without your passionate pursuit of effective communication. It would never have happened if you didn't patiently take the time to challenge me and help me grow as a communicator. Thank you for making the world a better place for me and everyone else to live in. Your words and your support of me will be ever in my soul.

And to everyone else who so generously backed the campaign:

Chris Mason, Brian Livaich, Tim Petrey, Claudia Vidal, Katie Switzer, Steve Hlabse, Steve Dale, Angelo Russo, Davide Viola, Thomas Chappell, Randy Green, George Bryant, Jeff Lawler, Michael Knulst, Kyle Lougnot, Dane Maxwell, Brandon Burchard, Timothy Dick, Vinnie Fisher, Thomas Matzen, Pamela Savino, Shannon Graham, Andy Humphrey, Annabelle Beckwith, Albert Martinez, Barry Kleiman, Frank Mendoza, Shane

Fielder, Sonny Tran, Brea Starmer, Susan McVea, Erick Magana, Iron Wil Becker, John Thompson, Scott Lucas, "Big" Chris Senkeresty, David Van Deman, Miguel Jones, David Conway, Jeeva Sam, Ryan Chute, Nate Kaminski, Shawn Cartwright, Adam LaFaber, Will Hurst, John Higham, Jeanie Holzbacher, Angie deBorja, Jeff Cool, Susan Cheek, Mary Ann Schneider, Max Bernstein, Lea Swanson, Sushee Perumal, Eric Butts, Justin Pickering, Wade Ellett, Jeff Brewer, Lori Gorrell, Cedric Crumbley, Christine Schlonski, Tim May, Todd Giannattasio, Alicia Schmitt, Paul Edwards, Diogène Ntirandekura, Amy Petrillo, Shanna Brown, Jason Hein, Brande Weber, Louann Vu, Marisa Cali, Bailee Szuter, John Kuder, Katherine Banfield, George Kalantzis, Alex Makarski, John Stiles, Billie Streets, David Ramsey, Betsy Aguilar, Jarrod Souza, Sean Scott, Amir Pozderac, Andrew Kaplan, Stephanie Jue, Jesse Krieger, Curtis Riley, David Foley, Lorna Moon, Mike Roderick, Ashley DeLuca, Paul Docampo, and Jeff Leshay.

You are all some of the best friends a guy could wish for. I could write some pretty amazing and hilarious stories about our times together, but that would end up being another book in itself, so please just know how much I appreciate you being in my life. Because you decided to bet on me and help me make this dream come true, tens of thousands of people will be impacted by this book. I will never forget how you helped make this dream possible for me.

And for every single other person who shared the posts about my book, told friends about it, and to YOU, the reader, holding this book in your hands, thank you for trusting me with your most precious asset: your time. I promise you that I have given you every last drop of goodness and truth that I can in this book. Thank you for buying this book and for choosing to invest in your communication skills.

I believe with all my heart that when we improve our communication skills, and truly learn to speak from the goodness of our hearts, that the world becomes a better place. You are the one creating the world around us, just as much as I am. So thank you for making it the beautiful and wonderful place that it is. I appreciate you.

Why Communication Matters

Thank you for picking up a copy of this book.

My intention in writing this book is to empower you to live a rich and powerful life that knows no limits. Let me tell you, writing it wasn't as easy as I would have wanted it to be. I'm just like you.

I have fears and insecurities, and if I would have focused on those, this book would never have been written. While I believe that all of us have a book inside of us, I'm not naive enough to believe that everyone will put in the work to create something that has the potential to outlast them.

Legacy is something that many people talk about, but in reality, our legacy is pointless to us. When I'm gone, I'll be buried in the ground somewhere, or maybe be sitting in a jar as a pile of ashes, and my "legacy" won't matter one damn bit to me.

So what is the point of focusing on legacy? Does it even matter? As someone who studies the stoic philosophers (Marcus Aurelius is one of my favorites) I tend to follow their advice when it comes to this life and the afterlife.

Recently, as I was reading Ryan Holiday's book *The Daily Stoic* (which I highly recommend)), I came across a meditation that really grounded me as it relates to my legacy. Essentially, what I learned from that passage in Ryan's book was this:

My legacy is meaningless if I'm both foolish enough and arrogant enough to think that it's something I will personally enjoy. And while I plan to live to be at least 120 years old, it doesn't matter how long I can stretch out my existence here on Earth as it relates to my legacy. I'm going to die just like you.

While that may sound like a morbid thing to say at the beginning of this book, it's actually something I find quite hopeful and grounding. Legacy is for and about everyone who comes after us. It's not something we'll be able to hold up as some kind of trophy.

Just like I read Marcus's book and received his wisdom centuries after he died, I truly hope that there will be people who get to enjoy this work of mine and find it valuable in their daily lives. I also hope that all the other work I'm doing in my life will stand the test of time and create a foundation for my great, great, great, great grandchildren.

Every day, I wake up and tell myself, "Esta es el momento perfecto," which means: This is the perfect moment. It reminds me that this is the perfect time to take action on what matters. It's the perfect time to tell someone that you love them and care about them. It's the perfect time to change the course of your life and leave a bigger dent in the universe before you check out.

So with all that said, the reason I decided to write this book is twofold:

First, I believe that communication is one of the foundational pieces required for a leader to achieve entrepreneurial success (and success in life in general as well).

Second, because I truly believe that everyone would be wise to consider writing a book and sharing their story. The world becomes more empathetic and connected when we take time to openly share with others.

I don't know about you, but I want my son and the generations that follow him to live in an increasingly better world. Despite what the flavor of the day is on the "news" (aka entertainment channels), I truly believe that the world is becoming a better place.

This isn't a pie-in-the-sky dream; it's actually a belief that is backed up with extensive research. In Steven Pinker's book *The Better Angels of Our Nature: Why Violence Has Declined*, he lays out a very clear and convincing data set that shows how our world is getting better.

Based on that book and other research I've done, I believe that violence began to decrease and empathy for others began to increase the day Johannes Gutenberg invented the modern printing press. That day, in the year 1440, I doubt that Johannes Gutenberg had any idea how impactful it would be.

Books change the world.

They change the world because they allow us to view things from another perspective. They allow us to communicate new ideas in great depth. Instead of asking a friend to sit and talk with us for 10 – 12 hours straight, while we are required to only listen and not respond, we now have the luxury of sharing all that information in a book that can be read at their leisure, bit by bit.

For those of you who have ever had your own garden, you know that a gentle rain is much safer and better for your plants than a torrential storm or flash flood. Gentle rain nourishes your plants, whereas the flash flood may destroy everything in one pass.

When we write a book, we get to drip the information into someone else's head at a slow pace, just like the gentle rain helps your garden grow. There have been a few times in my 20+ year career as an entrepreneur I have received compliments that stuck with me. They were both moments where I was truly proud of my work and also able to receive encouragement from those I appreciate and trust.

The first time was when my good friend Tori Reid said this to me:

"Reading your emails feels just like we're having a cup of coffee together. You feel so warm and approachable."

The second time was just recently when Wycliff Maina, one of my online family members who reads my email newsletters each week, wrote back to me and said this:

"Thanks for your rich life insights. Sometimes when reading your emails, I feel like you are there face to face addressing me and I must admit that is incredible."

I have to agree with Wycliff. It is incredible. The fact that we have the ability to put our words down on paper and share them with others is a truly amazing gift.

I'm sharing these two simple stories with you because I want you to realize that you too have the ability to care for, influence, and lead those around you with amazing communication. I believe with all my heart that excellent communication is the key to success in all areas of life.

When we're able to clearly communicate our intentions, where our heart is, and what we want to accomplish, it allows those around us to connect more deeply. As you'll learn throughout this book, I believe that entrepreneurship is servant leadership.

True entrepreneurs make a difference in the world by creating lasting impact. They make a difference by showing up and serving their audience at the highest level. While possible, I believe it's incredibly difficult to serve others well without having mastered communication.

This book is the summation of 20+ years of my journey to discover, learn, and apply the principles of communication. While I realize that my work in learning communication will never be 100% complete, I do feel confident that you will find incredible value in this book.

Communication affects everything. Our relationships, our team building efforts, our marketing, our sales, nearly everything comes down to communication. The principles and tools I will share with you here are ones I've learned from much wiser people than me. I've tested them, adjusted and improved on some of them, and done my absolute best to make them instantly applicable for your life.

I promise you that if you start implementing these tools, you will have the ability to impact more people in a positive way. You'll also have the opportunity to deepen your relationships with those around you that you love. As you read through the following pages, I have one recommendation for you:

Be open to trying these new tools and approaches.

Even if they seem silly or difficult to try at first, I'm absolutely certain that they can change your life. So when you learn a new tool, give it a try. You never know how it might change your life. And more importantly, you never know how it might impact the lives of those around you that you love and care for.

Improved communication is the answer you've been searching for in so many areas, so together let's give it a try. I promise you that I will do everything in my power to serve you and improve your life in the following pages.

If you choose to invest in yourself as it relates to your communication, I know that you'll be pleased with the result. Communication is everything, and I'm going to do everything I can to teach you more about it.

With all my love,
Gabe

Getting the Most Out of This Book

Before your dive in, I want to ensure that you are able to get the maximum value out of this book. I've created a resource guide, along with bonus videos that accompany this book. You can visit https://atomicwords.com/resources to get your free copy of the bonuses. Or just scan the QR code below:

There is a three-minute-long video on the resources page that, if you watch it, will help you take the first step towards delivering impactful communication. So go watch that now before you proceed. I promise you it will be worth the few extra minutes.

SECTION I

THE FOUNDATION

Foundational principles are what help us understand the path forward in any new skill, or any skill we're working to improve.

In this first section, I'm going to share the foundations that I've discovered over the course of the past two decades of work in communication.

I'm excited to share them with you, so let's dive right in.

CHAPTER 1

The Prism Effect

"Only the development of compassion and understanding for others can bring us the tranquility and happiness we all seek."
— The Dalai Lama

The Prism Effect

Have you ever held a prism in your hand? I have. To me it looks like a glass pyramid. When the light passes through it, the rays of light are split into a rainbow of beautiful colors. This image is probably most famous because Pink Floyd used it on their album *The Dark Side of the Moon*.

What I love about holding a prism is that on one side of the prism, there is normal light, and on the other side is an array of beauty and color. I believe that our perspective is The Prism Effect that we use to view the world around us. It affects how we interact with others, how we feel about them, and even how we feel about ourselves.

Let me share an example from my life that will illustrate this clearly.

I grew up in a family with one older sister and five younger brothers. Cody is my second to youngest brother and is one of the smartest, toughest, and kindest men I know. Even though he is over 10 years younger than me, I look up to him.

At the same time, he's one of my youngest brothers, so I feel a huge sense of responsibility for his well-being. I want to always give him the best advice and, of course, the best possible work I can give when he hires my team and me.

So my intentions, focus, and emotions around my choices as it relates to Cody and serving him and his business are a mix of love, care, and concern coupled with having deep respect for him as leader and businessman. With that frame of mind I'm deeply committed to serving him with amazing work that is on time.

That's how The Prism Effect first came to mind for me.

When I think about any one of my clients (and I believe that my team members are my internal clients), I ask myself, "If this was my brother Cody or my sister Heather, how would I treat them at this moment?" As I reflect back now with a little more wisdom, I feel like I've really dropped the ball in this area of my life in the past. Unfortunately, I haven't always viewed my team members and clients, along with my friends, in this light. While I think it's pretty normal to have a season of arrogance and narcissism in our lives, I regret that this season in my life was longer than it should have been.

I'm now deeply committed to using The Prism Effect every day in every way possible. You can achieve this powerful new perspective too. The specific shift and state change I'm recommending for you will help you hold yourself and your team to a higher standard of client service. I strongly believe that as entrepreneurs and leaders we must become great at showing care and empathy in our words and tone.

The true inspiration behind The Prism Effect is from a principle that one of my mentors, Brian Kurtz, talks about. He calls it 100/0. When we choose to go 100% of the way in a relationship, we are choosing to serve the other person at the highest level. Not expecting anything in return, and truly investing in relational reciprocity (not shallow transactional "reciprocity"), is what Brian teaches and is all about.

When I first heard his concept of 100/0, I intellectually got it, but I didn't truly understand it in my heart. It wasn't until I realigned my focus into serving at the highest level did it truly click. Once I understood that it was my job to go above and beyond in service, 100/0 made perfect sense to me, and the Universe delivered The Prism Effect to me.

I believe The Prism Effect can solve nearly all the problems that we face in business, and I also believe that it can solve almost all the problems in the world. There are too many "leaders" in our world right now who believe that trash talking and bullying are effective forms of communication. They aren't.

When we think about the perspectives of others, and when we truly show regard for them in the same way we would a dear loved one, then we are operating with a heart of service. In my personal experience, approaching a relationship with this perspective allows us to use the tone of voice and words that are aligned with our heart of love and service.

Years ago, when I was taking a very brief break from full-time entrepreneurship, I was working in an auto repair shop. It was part of a large chain that you drive past every day if you live in the United States, and it was truly one of the best learning experiences I've ever had. And interestingly enough, working there ultimately led me to create my first million-dollar product, Copywriter Today. Copywriter Today is a content subscription service that allows our clients to have an unlimited stream of fresh content for their marketing purposes.

When I started working at the auto repair shop, my manager, John, taught me how to truly listen to what the customers wanted. He used to say, "Just sell them what they came in for, Gabe!" He also taught me how to resolve conflicts with customers by just listening to them. While John had spent over 30 years in the auto industry at that point, he had managed to not become one of the bad guys.

I remember one day when one of the mechanics in the shop made a nearly fatal mistake and didn't properly tighten and check the torque on the lug nuts on a BMW he had just put new tires on. The customer had just returned from a deployment in Iraq.

This mechanic's nickname was Hulk. He was big and strong, and generally a decent enough guy to work with. The odd thing about this day is that there were two contrasting situations that occurred.

The first customer, the veteran, had an $80,000 BMW, and Hulk seemed more interested in the car than his work. When we received an angry call from the customer a couple hours later, my manager, John, lost his temper and was screaming at Hulk. The customer had been on the highway and lost one of the wheels.

He had a near-death accident and was rightfully upset. The way John reacted was obviously not the way to communicate with anyone, but I did understand why John was so angry. Hulk hadn't been paying attention and nearly killed one of our customers.

I remember John talking about our customer and saying, "He survived Iraq but he nearly died from Hulk's terrible work!"

Oddly enough, right after putting tires on the BMW, Hulk had put new tires on my beater car as well. He drove it around the block for me and double checked everything. Fortunately for me, he did excellent work on my car. None of my wheels fell off on the highway. I didn't have a near-death experience.

As I reflected on this experience last year before I even knew I was going to write this book, I realized that this was The Prism Effect in action. Hulk hadn't connected the fact that the other customer should have been treated like a brother or friend that he loved and cared about. But Hulk *did* connect the dots on my car. It was easier because we worked together, but I could tell he genuinely cared and wanted to do a great job for me. His perspective ultimately caused safety for me and near death for the other guy.

I believe that our perspective matters more than we realize. So next time you're faced with a situation where your attitude or the other person's attitude isn't the greatest, ask yourself this question:

"If they were a loved one, how would I treat them at this moment?" Or as one of my dear friends Pamela Savino asks in her book *Soar, "What would love do?"* Those are the questions that we can ask to put The Prism Effect into practice every day.

Sometimes You Have to Love Them and Let Them Go:

As much as I wish that we could love every client and everyone around us for the rest of time, it's not realistic. Let's use my family as a real and accurate example again.

I have a few family members that are just toxic for me to be around. I love them, but it's really unhealthy for us to spend too much time together. We just don't connect energetically, and it's a strain to be around them. I actually develop a sore throat when I'm around one of them for too long. I guess that's my body's way of warning me that the relationship is toxic.

I also (and I know I'm probably not the only one) have a family member that lies to me once in a while. I still love them but I can't work closely with them because I don't trust them like other members of my family who are honest with me no matter what. So I want to love all the clients I can, and I also know we will need to love some people from a distance because they are not trustworthy enough for us to work closely with them.

This mindset and the stories here are important to me because they outline how I want to show up in the world and treat those around me. Not every relationship is what we want or need, but even in those times when we know things need to change or even end, we can still be direct and kind when we part ways or slow down a relationship.

One thing I do with both those who lie to me and those trustworthy people like my brother Cody is, with the intention of love, challenge them periodically on their ideas and choices. I'll call them out gently on things they say that are bullshit.

Why do I choose positive confrontation in both relationships? Because I believe it's one of the most important ways that we love people. I strongly believe that positive confrontation is one of the healthiest forms of communication. It's also one of our guiding principles at my company Business Marketing Engine. So with both our clients and team members we love on, and also with those we have to conclude services with, we can lovingly challenge and confront them from time to time. When we confront anyone, we should begin from a place of love and service to them. If we state that intention of love and service before we confront them, we could make such a positive impact in their life by challenging them in a healthy way.

Going forward I'd encourage you to treat your clients and team members like your dearest loved ones by using The Prism Effect. When we hold the prism up and look through it, everyone we see around us suddenly is recognizable and beautiful in their own way because we see our loved ones in our clients.

You get to create the world you live in, so why not make it a beautiful place? Your world can be full of love, colors, joy, and healthy communication. All you have to do is use The Prism Effect every day.

Putting it into practice:

Write down three people or groups you dislike. Ask yourself where that perception came from and see if it is objective.

Write down things you want to change about your perception and relationships with those people.

Put these notes somewhere where you'll see them every day for a week.

After a week, see if your perspective and perceptions of others have changed.

Recently, as I finished the final touches on this book, I discovered that I had been missing an area in my life where I needed to apply The Prism Effect. Had I not taken time to reflect on this, I could have damaged a very important relationship and simultaneously lost out on millions of dollars of opportunities.

To hear this story, and to also see if you may be making the same mistake I was, make sure you have your copy of the bonuses that are available to you at https://atomicwords.com/resources. Or just scan the QR code below:

CHAPTER 2

The Wisdom Triangle

*"Wisdom is not a product of schooling but
of the lifelong attempt to acquire it."*
— Albert Einstein

In the middle of summer in 2020, my son and I decided to take a road trip from Ohio to Montana and do some camping. The reason for that was because 2020 wasn't exactly the year that anyone on the planet Earth planned for. With the COVID pandemic hitting hard in all areas of the world, the family cruise we'd planned to take got canceled. While I was disappointed at first, I chose to be grateful for the opportunity.

My son was eight years old at the time, and I knew that this would not only be the perfect time to get away from the rest of the world; I also knew that this was summer number eight of 18 that I had with him before he'd move on to adulthood. Being a father is something that I've dreamed about since I was my son's age at eight or nine years old, and so I never take for granted the time that I have with him. Every moment we get to spend together is truly magical.

And so while the world seemed to be burning down, according to the entertainment channels that label themselves "news," I got to experience one of the most magical and amazing summers of my life. I believe that the only reason that I'm blessed to be able to make that statement is because I've been striving for wisdom for years.

Einstein had it right in his quote. Wisdom isn't really an arrival point in your life; it's more of a journey of creating a principled approach to finding it. I hadn't fully realized this until one night when my son and I were sitting at the campfire, having a deep conversation about life. We were tired out from hiking up the mountain that day, and I was enjoying a beer. He was eating an incredibly burned marshmallow, just the way he likes them.

Out of nowhere he shared a story about someone else in his life who kept making the same mistakes and kept forgetting things. As we talked about this person, he shared with me that they read tons of books all the time. He didn't understand how they could read a lot but still act in a foolish manner. As I was sitting and listening to my son share this story, the concept of the Wisdom Triangle came to me. I held up both hands and made a triangle shape using my thumbs and index fingers.

I then explained to him that the wisdom triangle is made up of three corners. In the lower left is knowledge. The lower right point is experience. On the top point is wisdom. You cannot achieve wisdom unless you have both knowledge and experience. Those alone aren't enough either though. Your upward focus must be on discovering the pinnacle of wisdom. Wisdom doesn't just come to us naturally. We have to invest time and energy in deep thought.

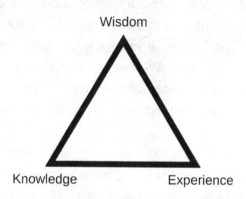

Taking time to reflect on what you know, and then comparing that to the empirical data that experience brings us is the first step. When you take time for deep reflection on both points of your knowledge and experience, you can then ask yourself, "What does this mean, and what should I do with that meaning?" That is the path towards wisdom.

Asking ourselves big, impossible questions is also something that I've found to be incredibly valuable. Whatever higher power designed and created our brains made them so that they can process information consciously and unconsciously.

This is incredibly valuable because if you ask yourself the same big hard question on a daily or even weekly basis, eventually your mind (after passing that question through some of your 86 billion brain cells a few times) will come back to you with a solid answer.

Your mind can actually turn something over trillions of times in just a matter of a few days or weeks. While in today's world we are beginning to have access to supercomputers that can mirror the performance of parts of the human mind, we don't yet have a computer that can achieve all the nuanced thinking that our brains can.

I also feel it's foolish to discount the power of divine influence on our lives as well. Supercomputers can do crazy things, but they don't have the human element that we have (at least not yet). Our intellect (our brain's computing power), coupled with our own spirit's intuition, and hooked up to the Universe's knowledge can (if we let it) lead to incredible amounts of wisdom. It's our job to cultivate wisdom.

As I've studied the great religions of the world, Eastern philosophy, and the words of the stoics, I've noticed a repeating pattern. All of these different belief systems and philosophies put a very high importance upon the practice of meditation.

Gaining knowledge, gaining experience, and then taking time to chew on and reflect upon the knowledge we have is something that produces incredible results in the long run. If you don't already have a daily habit of meditation, silence, and contemplation, I'd strongly encourage you to start implementing that right away.

I have yet to meet a truly successful entrepreneur and leader who doesn't practice some form of meditation in their daily lives. As I said earlier, becoming wise is not an arrival point; it's more of a daily practice. I also believe that wisdom can fade. If we don't keep the two foundational points of knowledge and experience sharp, then we'll miss out.

Knowledge from 20 years ago may or may not serve you well anymore. It will only serve you well if you continue to increase your knowledge in that area, apply it through real-life experiences, and then seek out the wisdom you need.

The Wisdom Triangle is a symbol that the Universe gave me in that moment on how to find and develop wisdom. Just like I shared it with my son, I want to share it with you. If you take your hands and make a triangle with your thumbs and index fingers, you can now look through that viewfinder and see the world around you.

Wisdom gives us the ability to view the world through our knowledge and experience lens. It should allow us to prepare for the future and learn from the past. It should also ideally help us be more objective and rely on more empirical data whenever possible.

Sometimes I see myself or others around me relying on just their knowledge. This approach leads to painful failures. In my first business I thought I knew it all because I'd read all the books on business and I figured that was enough. The problem was that I didn't actually have the experience to make wise choices in certain areas of that venture. Ultimately, my failure to utilize The Wisdom Triangle led me to lose a multimillion-dollar construction company during the housing market crash.

I "knew" it all back then in my twenties, and because of that a lot of people got hurt. It's one of the failures that I've forgiven myself for, and it's also one of the failures that I hold dear as a gift because it gave me the experience that ultimately led me to the wisdom I have today. It's also that kind of hard-earned wisdom that allows me to help so many of my clients overcome the challenges they face in their businesses every day.

When wisdom is properly cultivated, it should give us the confidence and ability to not react in the moment when something challenging occurs. When we intentionally use The Wisdom Triangle in every area of our lives and our businesses, we are able to show up with more love and service to others.

Why is this?

Because when you have wisdom, you have confidence in yourself. You have confidence in your knowledge and your experience. This confidence only truly comes when you have all three pieces in place. Knowledge, experience, and wisdom that comes from thoughtful introspection.

The deep work of life and entrepreneurship is not coming up with your next business idea. The deep and important work comes from looking inside ourselves and asking, "How can I take the gifts of wisdom I have and make the world around me a better place?" Wisdom is a hard-earned asset that makes you more valuable as an entrepreneur. It saves you and your team pain and failure. It helps you serve your clients at the highest level if you continually work to develop it.

Recently, I was speaking with a long-time client of mine who had to redeploy (fire) an employee because they had chosen to not do their job. Although in the moment it's one of the worst parts of my job, I've successfully redeployed hundreds of people over the years. I also help my clients redeploy team members that should be elsewhere.

In my experience, and with the knowledge that I have acquired over two decades as an entrepreneur, I have the wisdom to know that redeploying people is often the best way to serve them. When we don't let someone go when we should, we are actually hurting them, our teams, and ourselves.

So although it's one of the jobs I like the least in the moment, I still redeploy those that are no longer a fit for my team. I help my clients do the same because the servant leader entrepreneurs that I work with have big hearts. It's hard for them to let go of someone they invested so much in and had high hopes for.

In this case, my client knew they had to let this person go, and they did. It wasn't a pleasant experience, but nothing explosive happened. Then, a few weeks later, this ex-employee started drunk texting my client all sorts of threats and hateful things.

My client (who has been in business for over a decade) has wisdom. She sent one professional reply and then chose to disengage from the conversation. Wisdom tells us that engaging and escalating the upset person could lead to unfortunate consequences. Instead of reacting, my client acted with wisdom because this was not their first time redeploying a team member to other opportunities.

That is how wisdom is applied. Use your knowledge, use your experience, and then reflect on what you should learn from both. It's only when we use The Wisdom Triangle consistently that we can go from a place of knowledge to a place of knowing (aka wisdom).

This story also reminds me of one of the guiding principles we have at Business Marketing Engine. Our seventh principle states:

Challenges Are OK, Emergencies Are Rare – We believe that unless someone is bleeding or actually dying that we aren't experiencing a true emergency and we can take time to think, plan, and execute well. When necessary, we take The Matches Out of the Other Person's Hands.

Wisdom allows us to be responsive and not reactive. Rarely (unless as our seventh guiding principle states) is there actually an emergency that requires reactive and frantic behaviors and decision making. We almost always have the time to stop, think, and apply the hard-earned wisdom we have to the situation we're in.

While this is a simple foundational lesson, I strongly recommend that you take time to consider it. I'd encourage you to set aside a "wisdom hour" for yourself each week and take time for quiet reflection. No phone, no TV, maybe just a quiet place in your house, or maybe a quiet walk outdoors will work for you. For me, walking outside in nature is one of the best ways to reflect. There's a lot of science that points to the fact that when we are outside walking, the activity and the stimulation do incredibly wonderful things to our brains and health overall.

Regardless, whatever structure you put in place, stick to it for four weeks in a row and then see how you feel. Do you have more confidence in yourself? Do you feel more at peace? Or maybe, you start to feel uncomfortable because there are some things that you need to address that you've been ignoring. Whatever comes up for you, don't push it away. Sit with it and choose a curious and open state of mind.

Prayer, meditation, and thoughtful silence are some of the secret weapons that all great entrepreneurs use to guide them forward in their pursuit of wisdom. Wisdom tells us that slowing down will give us the time and space to thoroughly process through what's happening around us and allow us to make the best decision we can.

While taking action is an absolute key part of success, taking unplanned action often leads to expensive learning experiences. While we can learn from and value the times that we took that approach, it's not something that should be repeated over and over. I remember years ago when I first heard the international bestselling author John Maxwell share about his "thinking chair." He spoke about how each day he takes time to sit quietly and think.

Jeff Bezos of Amazon has a similar mindset. He doesn't believe in waking up crazy early like some entrepreneurs do. He takes time to ease into his day, have breakfast with his family, and I've also read that he will block out one to two hours per day for alone time just for thinking.

You can't conquer complex things and you can't grow your business without wisdom. Insanity is doing the same thing and expecting different results, right? So in order to grow and change, I'd strongly recommend that you set aside time to think. Setting new thought patterns, considering what's working and not working, and reflecting on who you are and how you want to show up in this world is some of the most important work you'll ever do.

Putting it into practice:

Take time right now to block out thinking time as a recurring appointment at least once a week in your calendar.

Also, I'd encourage you to take time today for quiet reflection. If you just take 15 minutes right now, you'll have the opportunity to deepen your wisdom and uncover the truth you need in this season of your life.

When you sit down to think, start by asking yourself these questions and then write down what comes to you. Ideally, you should use an offline device for notes (like pen and paper or a device on airplane mode) so you don't get distracted with notifications and other noise.

Ask yourself:

1. What am I most proud of in my life right now?

2. What things do I need to improve on personally?

3. What knowledge and experience do I need to gain in order to serve and impact more people around me?

I have a special section in the bonus resources focused on how to apply The Wisdom Triangle to your life. So if you haven't already grabbed your bonuses, head over to https://atomicwords.com/resources to get your free copy. Or just scan the QR code below:

CHAPTER 3

The Confidence Core

"Because one believes in oneself, one doesn't try to convince others. Because one is content with oneself, one doesn't need others' approval. Because one accepts oneself, the whole world accepts him or her."
— Lao Tzu

As much as I wish that confidence was something we're born with, I don't believe that to be true anymore (at least in most cases). I'm an incredibly confident salesperson, writer, and entrepreneur and yet in other areas of my life I'm fearful. While admitting that doesn't really make me feel that tough and strong, I've decided that it's better to be honest and vulnerable than it is to sell you a load of crap.

I first noticed my lack of confidence in certain areas when I was 16 years old. I was already selling websites and doing construction and remodeling projects on the side, so I was clearly confident in some things.

The challenges started popping up for me when it came to dating and approaching the opposite sex. I remember the first time I bought a girl that I liked flowers. I took a lot of time to plan it out. I figured that giving her flowers (despite the fact we weren't dating or in any kind of serious relationship) was a great first move.

So I bought her flowers and a card and walked into the church youth group meeting early. I found her, awkwardly walked up to her, said, "Here. These are for you," and handed her the flowers.

I figured I had it all nailed down...

Well, clearly, that is not how to approach some girl you like. She turned red, laughed, and then her friend laughed at me too. She ended up leaving the flowers sitting on a table and never came back for them.

I was crushed.

In that moment, I realized that I had no idea what I was doing. It was incredibly embarrassing, and I didn't even know what I had done wrong. Unfortunately, that experience along with a few other cringe-worthy moments shaped my lack of confidence early on as a teenager as it related to meeting and talking to women.

The good news is that I have been blessed with some amazing women who, over the years, have helped me overcome some of my fear and lack of confidence. The even better news is that my life partner, Rachel, saw how awkward and insecure I was when we first met and went the extra mile to show me the way to deep connection.

Now, thanks to her, I don't feel inadequate at all in that area of my life. We've had lots of long conversations and tried different ways to work together so that I don't feel insecure about any areas of my relationship with her. Before I met Rachel, I blamed myself for my lack of confidence in this area of my life.

What really baffled me was that I was *super confident* in so many areas of life, yet this one escaped me. By the time I was 25 years old I had already sold over 10 million dollars' worth of products and services. You'd think that with that kind of sales track record I could "seal the deal" with the opposite sex.

Unfortunately, confidence in one area doesn't necessarily translate to confidence in other areas. It wasn't until I set my intentions on writing this book that I finally uncovered the truth of where confidence originates.

The Confidence Core is something that I've witnessed in action thousands of times.

Early in my life I just didn't realize it was there. Until recently, when I did the deep internal and reflective work that it takes to uncover important truths, it was a mystery to me. Now that I've uncovered The Confidence Core, I personally believe that it is the truth for me and for almost everyone on the planet. Once I break this down for you, I want you to think about the areas you're confident in. I want you to think about the areas you're not confident in.

As you take time to reflect, I'm certain that this framework will not only illuminate new truths for you, but it will help you understand some of your past history too. So let's dive into The Confidence Core framework now.

In order to find confidence, you need the following key components:

First, you need a trusted advisor who has a servant's heart and truly cares about you.

Second, you need someone who teaches and shows you the way by example, not just by talking about things in theory.

And third, you need to practice their approach to get consistent results in your own life.

It's really that simple.

When I think about my confidence in sales, it reminds me of the time my grandfather took me to look at a prospective client's masonry project. When we arrived at the homeowner's house, the prospect explained that they needed their stone wall repaired.

My grandfather held out his hand, smiled, and said, "Just hand me your checkbook. I'll write in the amount, and we'll take great care of you!" He said it with a chuckle, but what blew me away is the prospect *did, in fact,* hand him her checkbook.

My grandfather was one of the first entrepreneurs to show me (not just tell me) that entrepreneurship is truly about servant leadership. In the end he wasn't asking for the prospect's checkbook to rip her off; he was saying with his smile, his tone, and eventually his words and deeds, that he would take great care of her.

If that had been the only time I saw my grandfather sell something, it likely wouldn't have been enough. Fortunately for me, he showed me how to look at blueprints, write up specifications, and figure out what things cost. For a guy who only had a third-grade education and could barely read or write, he did incredibly well. Over the years, I believe that my grandfather sold well over 100 million dollars in contracting services.

He also owned a restaurant, bowling alley, and investment properties. While he didn't always come out on top in every deal he made, he did, over time, get better at it and retired very comfortably with two homes and multiple boats, cars and trucks, and other toys that he enjoyed.

While his toys were something that he enjoyed, he would often look over at me during the workdays we spent together and say, *"You know, Gabe, we work hard so we can go fishing when we want to!"* That's really all my grandfather wanted from life by the time I was around. He loved spending time out on the water, sitting, fishing, and reflecting on life. If I close my eyes, I can still hear his voice and see his warm smile.

He also deeply valued the relationships in his life. He would walk through his hometown with me on sunny afternoons as we made our way to get some pie and ice cream at his favorite restaurant, and it would take us an hour just to get to where we were going.

Everyone knew him by name, and they all loved talking to him. He was someone that truly valued relationships. He's the one who inspired me to create our first guiding principle at Business Marketing Engine.

It says:

"Relationships First – We believe that relationships are more important than money. We show up and give our best work to all those around us. We listen first and then serve."

When my grandfather passed away, and I had the incredible honor and privilege to give his eulogy, there were hundreds of people in attendance. In that moment I understood at a deeper level that he truly walked the talk and showed up for all the people in his life that he led and cared about.

As I've taken time to reflect on the confidence I have, a huge majority of it came from my grandfather, Ray Arnold. He was that trusted advisor in my life with a servant's heart. He showed me the way to work hard, sell, serve, and love and help people every single day.

When I started practicing what he had demonstrated to me for so many years, it was easy to be confident. Even when things were shaky, I knew what to do because I'd seen him work through some incredibly tough times.

Right now you may be lacking confidence in your communication skills. Or, you might be lacking confidence in another area of your life as well. I want you to know that it's OK to feel unconfident. I felt that way when I started writing this book.

It was only after reading, studying, and watching some of my trusted advisors that I discovered that there was a framework and process that I could follow.

I wrote a few small books to start.

I practiced what I had seen others do.

And over time... I started to see that the processes that I had observed began to work for me too.

In my experience, you're going to have to do the same thing with communication and other new skills that you want to learn and gain confidence in. So with that in mind, I promise to walk you through as much as I possibly can as it relates to what I've learned about communication. This way you can rely on me to be the trusted advisor that shows you the way.

What I can tell you with absolute confidence is this:

When you practice these communication tools and processes on a consistent basis, you will find that your work is easier, and your stress is lower.

Too often in life we are trying to force things that don't work well. Other times we don't have the confidence or skills to achieve the results we want, so we become stressed and end up breaking things unintentionally. Whether we're breaking things inside our own business or hurting an important relationship, in the end, the costs are far greater than we can afford. That's why mastering communication is so important.

With efficient and effective communication we can clearly communicate, serve at the highest level, and make the world a better place. And that, my friend, is what I am all about. Serving you and making *your world a better place.*

Putting it into practice:

What is one area where you have amazing confidence and success? Who showed you the way?

What is one important area where you lack confidence? Where can you find a trusted advisor to show you the way?

Who in your life needs you as a trusted advisor? How can you give them the confidence they need?

If for some reason you don't already have the bonuses for this book, I'd encourage you to head over to https://atom-icwords.com/resources to get your free copy. Or just scan the QR code below:

In the bonus section for The Confidence Core I not only share how to find trusted advisors who can help you build confidence, but I also talk about how to identify those who should not be trusted. In my many years as an entrepreneur, I've run into my share of wolves in sheep's clothing that have cost me time and money that I didn't have to waste. I want you to be able to avoid those mistakes too. The Confidence Core tool actually came to me when I was doing deep reflection around a few people who, after I started working with them, turned out to be con artists.

The value of the lessons I learned was worth the price, but I'd rather you just get the lesson and skip the pain. So check out the bonus resources around The Confidence Core so you can benefit from my expensive lessons.

THE TOOLS

Having the right tools makes the job a lot easier, and it makes the quality of work we're producing much higher. It's not that it's impossible to dig a moat around your house with a spoon; it's just that it's a hell of a lot easier to do so with a big ol' excavator.

In this section I'm going to share with you the tools I've discovered, created, and used to improve my own communication skills. I also teach these tools to my team and clients, so they are tested processes that serve us all well. I'll use real life examples from my own life and my work with my team and clients.

The good news is that you get to start using these tools right away.

Don't worry, you won't be perfect on the first attempt, but let me tell you, using a big ol' excavator, no matter how unskilled you are, goes a lot faster than using the spoon you're used to digging moats with. So go ahead and give these a try right away! They will change your life, lower the stress and noise, and help you communicate at a deep and positively intense level.

But please remember this before we dive in:

Your heart's intention is louder than any words or tools you can use. So make sure you remember The Prism Effect before you begin any communication. Envision your audience as your dearest loved ones. That way you can come to the conversation with the right energy and the right intention. This simple approach has saved me so much heartache and so many mistakes, so I wanted to remind you again of it here as well.

We'll talk about how to make your communication and intentions even more powerful in this section, but for now, remember to show up to every conversation with love and care for the other person. That's truly the secret you need to ensure that these tools make an incredibly positive impact on you and those around you.

CHAPTER 4

The Magic A.R.C.

"A lack of clarity could put the brakes
on any journey to success."
— Steve Maraboli

In my experience, crystal clear communication builds trust. Unfortunately, most of us have never had a trusted advisor teach us what truly clear communication looks like.

I remember back when I was 19 years old and my construction business was growing rapidly. I was in a season where I was hiring rapidly, but I was still out in the field doing the work as well. I had recently been contracted to build some stone piers at the end of a driveway by a general contractor that I worked for periodically. When I met with him, he had shared the blueprints with me, the type of stone they wanted, and the due date that he needed the project done by.

It was a lot to take in during our brief 20-minute meeting, but I was very confident that I'd gathered all the information I needed to be successful. I asked my client if he had pulled all the permits and handled all the setup steps required, and he said yes.

The meeting was full of details and context, and while it wasn't the largest project I'd taken on by any means, there was definitely a lot to take in during our short time together. A few days later, I pulled up to the project with a mini excavator on my trailer and after unloading, I started digging at the spot that my client had marked out for me. This wasn't the first time I'd done excavation work, and so I was smoothly digging my way down into the earth.

I needed to dig down 42" below the driveway so we could pour solid concrete footers for the large piers we were going to build. I was focused on my work, and as I dug the bucket of the excavator into the earth, around a depth of 36", all of a sudden I heard a pop and then a hissing sound.

Almost instantly, I smelled natural gas, and I immediately shut down the excavator. I'd unintentionally dug through a two-inch gas line that was running from the road to the home that was at the other end of the driveway. While I had experienced digging through water lines and very small electrical lines before, I had never dug through a gas line before.

The dangerous part about ripping through a gas line is that one spark can, in a worst-case scenario, create a massive explosion, or, at best, a raging fire. Fortunately, I didn't get blown off my excavator that day.

I was able to carefully and slowly make my way into the hole I had dug and slowly and carefully use a clamp to squeeze off most of the flowing gas. I then called the utility company and my client to inform them of what had happened. Fortunately, everyone else involved was very understanding and I wasn't charged the regular fine that can often accompany this kind of error.

Now, as I look back on that situation, I realize that I could have been killed. Just as importantly, I look back and now realize that if I would have known about and used the tool I'm going to share with you called A.R.C. in my meeting with my client, I could have asked clearer questions, gotten better information, and not assumed that my client had already called to have the utilities marked for me.

That near-death experience, and other less-than-ideal miscommunications over my years of being an entrepreneur led me to realize that finding and creating clarity is something that is incredibly important.

If we want to achieve success in our lives and our businesses, and if we want to be successful in our leadership roles, making clearer and effective asks of those around us is critical. That is why I frequently use a tool I discovered called A.R.C.

A.R.C. stands for: Ask, Reason, Context.

Unfortunately, most of us were taught to communicate like CRAp, the reverse of ARC.

I was first introduced to this concept by my good and very wise friend Jay Crouch. He had hired me to help him market a new service he was offering to startups. During that process, he shared an article with me that he had written on his blog about how to communicate with technical team members.

Early on in the project I realized that Jay was one of the most articulate, intense, and thoughtful communicators I had ever met. Many of the concepts in this book have come from conversations I originally had with him.

And on a personal note, Jay, I am incredibly grateful for everything you've taught me as it relates to communication. So when you read this, I hope you realize how many people you've impacted by simply teaching me how to communicate more effectively.

So why do we need to use A.R.C.?

The reason is that most people naturally feel the need to start with a mind-numbing amount of context. I have met both men and women whose natural communication style is to first tell you *all the background information* before getting to the point of what they need.

While I understand that there are some instances when people need to process through things by talking them out, it is not the ideal information delivery method in most cases. And guess what communication is? It's the process of transferring information from one point to another. In our case here, it's the process of transferring information from one human to another.

The problem is that most people start with context. If you start with context, you end up brute forcing the listener's brain.

Brute forcing in the technical world is a term for when a bunch of computers try to attack one computer or website with millions of pieces of requests for information with the goal of taking it down or hacking the site.

Or, if you think about this in more ancient terms, when one army was attacking another army's city, they would often send hundreds of men and a battering ram to the city gate and simply pound on it long enough and hard enough until they broke it down.

When we speak with too much context first, the listener's brain is struggling to understand the ask and the _reason_ you are asking for their help. They are burdened with too many words (context) and they have no effective filter with which to categorize the words you're sharing with them.

You can often unintentionally cause mental and emotional stress in your listener when you take the approach of context first. If you stress your listener, then your message will get lost as their brain tries to protect itself first, and then sort out the information later (if they remember any of it).

Like I said earlier, using the wrong approach is what most of us were taught to do. CRAp is the result of not using A.R.C.

Here is a fictitious example of CRAp in motion:

Earlier today Rachel was working on sales handoff forms and she had to do about 12 of them in a row. That's because I sold a bunch of deals last Thursday night, and since they weren't urgent, she decided to do the forms this week for me. I think that there may have been an issue with the forms that we didn't plan for, so what I'm wondering, Dave, is if you can look at the forms and help me make some adjustments to one of the fields.

After reading that, do you clearly know what I need help with? Unless you are a mind reader, the answer is absolutely not! You have no idea what I need help with.

I just threw a lot of noise your way, and there was no clear ask. Yes, there were some vague requests, but they lacked specificity. That's how most people communicate by default, and it's taxing on the brain and highly ineffective.

Here's how we turn CRAp around to A.R.C.:

I know it's spelled wrong, but maybe this "A.R.C." is the verbal Noah's ark that will save us from a biblical flood of context that washes our brain out! Building an A.R.C. will save your communication!

Here's a clear A.R.C.

Ask: Dave, I need to ask you to add a field to the sales handoff form that indicates if a project management board needs to be created.

Reason: There are some projects that require it, and I want my assistant to know right away if that's the case.

Context: I discovered this when Rachel was doing handoff forms today, and she wasn't sure how to indicate which sales handoffs needed project boards.

Do you see how focused that ask is? It's **very clear** what I need so that the listener can organize all the following data contextually around the ask because the ask is stated first. This is how I ask all my team members to communicate when we need help with something.

I would strongly recommend that you use this tool exactly as I have outlined it. So when you need help, or need to delegate something, just approach it like this and fill in the blanks:

Ask: I want to achieve _____

Reason: The reason I need this is because _____

Context: Here are all the additional contextual pieces that are part of this ask.

When you write your next email, when you have your next verbal or video communication, use this format, and I promise you that you will very quickly achieve maximum velocity and maximum impact in your communication.

This works well professionally and personally as well. And while I don't advocate for every single conversation to be structured, I do believe that if you used this approach 80% of the time, you'd see amazing results.

There are, of course, free-flowing conversations and brainstorming sessions that need to happen. In my experience though, we need fewer of those brainstorming sessions than we may think. It's more important to have clear A.R.C. style conversations whenever possible so that we don't tire out our audience's brain needlessly. And to be clear, when I use the word "audience" here and in the rest of this book, I mean either an audience of one or an entire group of people with whom you are communicating.

There's also another hidden benefit of using A.R.C. when you communicate. It actually helps you to think more effectively and solve more problems independently. Doing the work up front to get clear about the ask you have is worth the effort because there are plenty of times when we start talking before we even know what we are truly asking for.

Our team holds a daily all-hands-on-deck team huddle, and I've found that this practice of using A.R.C. makes these meetings much more effective. When a team member or I have a problem we're trying to solve, framing it up using the Ask, Reason, and Context allows the entire team to very efficiently get to the root of the ask and start offering solutions.

How many times have you been in a meeting and after 15 – 20 minutes you still don't know what the point of the meeting is? This is all too common in the entrepreneurial world, and yet it is totally avoidable.

So let's use A.R.C. together right now:

Ask: I'd like to ask you to use A.R.C in your next email or instant message.

Reason: The reason is that if you put this into practice right away, it will stick with you.

Context: When I coach business leaders, I've found that they are able to learn the principles I teach must faster and retain them for much longer when they practice them immediately. So if you stop reading right now and send your first A.R.C. communication around a real ask you have, you'll remember how to use it.

Additionally, you'll see a very different type of response from your audience. They'll more quickly understand what you need from them. You'll also cut down the confusion time, which saves them time and energy. Conserving that time and energy is valuable to them personally, to the organization as a whole, and will allow them to reserve their energy for more important and challenging tasks.

My perspective is that using A.R.C. is a huge win win win. You get a better and faster response, your team members get clear direction, and they also save their time and energy for the organization and for their own personal lives and families too.

Putting it into practice:

Ask: Please use A.R.C. at least twice this week.

Reason: If you use it multiple times, you'll be able to see the immediate impact it makes.

Context: When a new team member is onboarded to our team, this is one of the very first things we teach them. It cuts down on communication overhead and saves their time and energy.

Give it a try! And let me know how it works for you. I'm always looking for feedback on how I can improve the communication tools we create and use.

To get a printable PDF that reminds you how to use A.R.C. in your daily life, head over to the bonus page for this book at https://atomicwords.com/resources or just scan the QR code below:

CHAPTER 5

Powerful Frames

"A lot of people in our industry haven't had very diverse experiences. So they don't have enough dots to connect, and they end up with very linear solutions without a broad perspective on the problem. The broader one's understanding of the human experience, the better design we will have."
— Steve Jobs

A few months ago, I woke up early and stumbled down the stairs to my back porch. When I started to walk out on the porch, there was a bright orange glow from the back yard. It was hazy, and I couldn't see the back tree line.

I could feel the heat as I opened the sliding door on the porch.

At first, I was surprised and a little startled.

I couldn't see clearly through all the haze and for a moment, I was beginning to wonder if something had caught fire...

I opened the door and all of a sudden…

Stop.

What if I stopped the story right there? What are you currently thinking was happening in my backyard at that moment?

Because I chose to frame the story with colors and haze and with a feeling of bewilderment, your imagination may have started to color in some details that I didn't actually share.

What were you thinking?

Was it a storm?

Was it a fire?

Was it something else?

When we begin a conversation, we have the ability to set things up so that we influence and frame the content that follows. Fortunately for me, the backyard was just full of fog and the bright morning sun was coming up in a radiant glow.

The frame that we choose to give to our audience affects how they view the subject matter. Oftentimes we incorrectly frame something because we aren't even aware of what a frame is, or how we use them consciously or unconsciously.

What I love about the Steve Jobs quote is that he identifies the gaps that many people have. They have those gaps in their thinking because they haven't been exposed to experiences that allow them to think bigger.

What's amazing though, is that when we use intentional frames, we can actually help our audience get broader perspectives. We can help them simulate experiences that will serve them and their thought processes well.

Now that we've introduced the concept of using frames, I'll share with you a few different frames that you may recognize, and a few other frames that you can use to improve the delivery of your message to your audience.

Ineffective Frames:

"We need to talk."

Do you remember hearing those words from a parent, a boss, a friend, a partner or loved one? If you're like most people I've discussed that phrase with, then you probably get nervous when you hear someone say that.

The "We need to talk" frame will put people in a fearful state.

When someone is operating out of fear, they aren't in receiving mode. They're not able to remain open and curious because they are gearing up for a tough conversation and they need to protect themselves. Even when you need to deliver difficult news, you can do so with a more productive frame.

"I can't believe you just did that."

Often this frame is used in a judgmental way when someone has made a big mistake. When you unintentionally bring judgment on someone else, you close off the possibility of free-flowing dialogue.

It's more effective to remain curious and open when you need to address something that happened. Observing is often much more productive than judging someone.

And think about it, do you feel accepted and comfortable freely sharing when someone questions your behavior in a negative manner? I know I don't.

"You can't do it that way."

When you frame any part of your conversation that way, you often will trigger the defiant four-year-old self of your audience. I know that some of my biggest successes were fueled by people telling me just that—that I couldn't do something that way. Or they'd say it was impossible, and I would immediately ignore them.

One story that comes to mind is when I was 18 years old, I was working with my grandfather, who taught me the masonry trade as a nine-year-old kid.

I was tuckpointing some brick under a stone step. (When you tuckpoint, you take fresh mortar that was just mixed and press it into the open gaps in the brick where old mortar has been removed or has deteriorated from age and weather.)

My grandfather said to me, "You won't be able to tuckpoint with the jointer you have. You can't do it that way." Of course, I thought I knew everything about everything, and being the arrogant kid I was, I said, "Yes I can. Watch me!"

My grandfather was just as hardheaded as I can be sometimes, so he left to go get the right tool, and meanwhile (even though he was half right), I figured out a way to do it with the tool I had.

I was hell bent on doing it my way, and honestly, it was mainly because he told me that I was doing it the wrong way. By the time he got back from getting me the right tool, I was done, even though I had to work twice as hard to use the wrong tool to do the job.

I would encourage you to consider a different approach next time you feel like saying "It can't be done that way" because in my experience you'll get a lot farther with better frames.

Effective Frames

When you realize that frames have an incredible influence on the content that follows them, I believe you'd be wise to start using them intentionally.

"Have you ever considered…"

If my grandfather had started off with this frame, I bet he'd have been able to influence my thinking more effectively:

"Have you ever considered using a different tool for that part of the project, Gabe?" There are a lot of frames that I've found to be much more effective when speaking to my audience, of one or many.

"I would encourage you to consider…"

This is a great one to use when you're giving advice or suggesting a different path. While your audience may not listen to what you have to say, the odds of them shutting down and not listening at all are much lower with this approach.

I remember earlier this year when I was meeting with a family member of mine who was incredibly upset about something that had happened in their life. They were venting to me, and they continued to use language that grouped me into a larger group of people that they were offended by.

Instead of using an ineffective frame, like "You can't include me in that group!" I decided to say, "I would encourage you to consider how that statement makes me feel, because I'm right here listening to you. I feel hurt by what you're saying because you're grouping me in with people that you say you hate right now."

Not surprisingly (because in my experience frames really do work well), my family member changed their language and stopped grouping me in with the other people that they were upset with. Regardless of how I said it, it was important to positively confront what was being said in the moment. However, if I would have been more combative and not framed up my statement the way I did, it would have most likely escalated the situation instead of calming it down.

If you think back to the last negative confrontation you had, do you think there is a more effective frame you could have used before responding with your thoughts? I know this may not feel natural at first, it wasn't for me, but when we intentionally choose our frames, we get to control the outcome in a very positive manner.

"Feel free to choose what you feel is best."

When we choose to frame our conversations like this, we are intentionally empowering our audience with the right to choose. As humans we need autonomy and freedom to choose. Instead of telling someone what they have to do, we can simply offer them the option and let them choose.

In my experience it's very difficult and highly ineffective to try and control another adult human. Yes, there are times we need to keep our children from running into the street, and physically controlling them is in their best interest. That period in our relationship to a child generally ends very quickly though when they get closer to their teenage years. In the end, people are free to choose what they want, so we should use that truth to serve and help them, and not try to butt up against them by telling them what they need to do.

"The problem I'm trying to solve…"

This is one of my favorite frames to use in business and it also works well personally. When you open your conversation with this frame, you immediately tune the audience's brain into a focused area. When you start off with "The problem I'm trying to solve is how to lower our customer refund rates," there is no ambiguity to your ask. It's clear what you need help with.

This frame is a shortcut for A.R.C. because it just gets straight to a specific ask around a problem you have. The other great thing about this frame is it taps into people's desire to help. I believe that one of our deepest human desires is to help others out and contribute in a meaningful way.

When we use this frame of "The problem I'm trying to solve," we very quickly tap into that amazing and powerful desire. Give this frame a try next time you have something you need help with, and watch your audience jump into help.

"My intention is…"

I really enjoy using many different frames, and this one ranks at the top for me because it's a double frame. When I open my conversation with "My intention is to serve and help you," I align my own heart, actions, and mindset towards serving my audience of one or many people. This frame also lets the audience know my true intentions.

I recently had a conversation with a client and used this frame in an effective manner. I'd just completed a strategic business and marketing plan for my client and presented it to him. While they were pleased with the overall results, he had questions about why part of the process cost so much. In that moment I was concerned that he didn't understand the value of what had been provided so far, and that they were going to ask for a refund or some kind of discount.

That is a common challenge that we face as entrepreneurs and leaders when we haven't properly communicated our process and our value up front. I realized when my client started voicing a few objections that I had missed a step in the earlier conversations we'd had.

Nearly every time I skip part of my own process, I eliminate the opportunity for effective and clear communication. While I'm glad to say that I do this very infrequently at this point in my career, there are still times where I slip up. In the moment I justify the behavior to myself by saying I'm saving time, and it will be faster and easier just to move ahead with something.

In reality, all I do is create more work for myself and my team later on. And undoing miscommunication is so much harder than just doing it right in the first place. So now my client didn't understand something, and it was my responsibility to resolve it.

I could tell that he was frustrated and I felt that at least part of their frustration was justified because I'd made a mistake in an earlier stage of the project. So I wrote him a detailed email, and in that email, I wrote this important line:

"My intention is to serve you at the highest level, and I want to do everything on my end to ensure your project is a massive success."

By simply stating my true heart's intentions, I was able to diffuse what could have been a messy situation. And the results were very positive. My client immediately started trusting me again, and they decided to move forward with the next phase of the project.

In that example stating my heart's intentions and sending clear communication only required that I invest about 10 minutes of my time. The result was that I was able to generate nearly $30,000 of revenue for my company that day.

That's just one simple example of what happens when you frame up your communication with sincere and service-focused intentions. When we invest in clear and effective communication, everyone wins.

Think about it from your perspective. If someone comes to you and expresses that they simply want to help you and do what's best for you, it's difficult to ignore them, isn't it? As humans we are incredibly adept at determining when someone is being sincere or when they are just saying the words without a true heartfelt intention behind it.

So don't worry about how your intention-framed statements are received. Don't worry about saying it perfectly. Focus instead on getting grounded and centering yourself before writing or saying those words. If you truly intend to serve and care for someone, and if you truly mean what you say when you frame up a conversation with your honest intentions, your audience will hear and understand your words and your heart.

One great way to implement this approach is to look ahead at your planned conversations for the day or week and write a list of your intentions. This is something that I did occasionally over the years, but recently, it's become a consistent habit because of a great tool that I use every day.

My friend Alex Charfen created a planner for entrepreneurs called the Momentum Planner. The very first section of the daily planner that I use asks, "What are your intentions for the day?" That simple question helps me align my head and my heart each morning. I take just a few moments and I write out my intentions for the day.

Sometimes they are unique to the things I have going on that day, and other times I write similar things to previous days.

Here's an example from one of my recent journal entries:

My intention today is to:

- Be present for myself throughout the busyness of my schedule.
- Connect with Rachel and my son at a deeper level.
- Serve my team and my clients at the highest level.
- Serve my clients by selling them the right solution, for them.

Not only does setting daily intentions help me get focused on what matters; I also know from experience that these intentions are heard by the Universe or whomever you call your higher power. It's not by accident that those who set intentions for their days and for their years almost always achieve and surpass the outcomes they are aiming for.

Now as you think about your own situation, let's explore an example scenario together:

Imagine that you have a meeting with a new client named Judy today. Think about what you really want to do in your meeting. I know from personal experience that the best way to grow your business is by serving your clients (both internal and external clients) at the highest level.

With that in mind, what is your intention for your time with Judy today? If you write that down, you can open your meeting with the frame, "My intention today, Judy, is to serve you and focus on xyz."

One strong encouragement I have for you as you read this is to realize that this frame is incredibly powerful. Like I mentioned earlier in the chapter, if someone were to use it without sincerity, it could be even more damaging than any negative frame could be.

Manipulating someone in a less than honest manner will hurt you more than it hurts them in the long run. Obviously, you're free to choose; however, my strong encouragement is that you never use this (or honestly any of these tools in this book) with negative intentions.

Important Emotional Safety Frames

Last year I had an unexpected and very unfortunate error occur. One of my team members was updating a Google Ads campaign for one of our clients. We'd been getting really good results for our client, and Google's AI on their platform suggested some keyword changes and keyword bid modifications. This is all very commonplace in our work, and generally, when we make the suggested changes, that's all that gets applied. Just a small adjustment to the detailed level of a campaign.

In this case, there was some kind of error on Google's Ads platform, and not only did the changes to the keywords get made, but it also automatically adjusted the daily budget for the campaign. Because this error occurred, my client's daily budget was set to $9,000 per day. Now, while we have helped a few clients spend at this level before successfully, this client was not ready for that level of advertising yet.

Unfortunately, we didn't catch the platform error that occurred until the next day. When we did, we also discovered that there had been additional errors in the Google Ads platform earlier in the month that had been missed as well. All told, the errors cost our client an extra $30,000 in ad spend, which was 400% of their monthly budget.

When I realized this I had a bad feeling in the pit of my stomach. I knew that this error happened on our watch, and I immediately felt bad about the whole situation. At first, for a moment or two, I was angry that it happened (as I think many of us would be). I wondered how I could make it right before the client saw it.

Fortunately, I've faced some pretty serious challenges over the years, and this one only knocked the wind out of me for a few minutes. Once I had stabilized emotionally and mentally, I knew what I had to do.

Thinking about how to resolve it before telling my client is not one of my proudest moments, but in just a matter of minutes I reminded myself, as I often do, that it's always the right time to do the right thing. I called my client and took full ownership for the error. I let them know that it was an error on Google's end, but because it happened on our watch, I was going to take responsibility for resolving the error with Google and covering any financial fall out that impacted my client.

In that moment, my client could have ripped me a new one, but instead he chose to be incredibly kind and gracious. After I hung up, I thought a lot about how he responded because I've had the opposite kind of response before (as many of us have had). Instead of screaming at me and freaking out, my client trusted me and communicated with incredible respect and calm amidst what was a bad-looking situation.

I believe that he responded this way for two reasons:

First, because he's an amazing human and someone I will always have respect for regardless of whether we are still working together.

Secondly and just as importantly, I believe that what we put out into the Universe comes back to us tenfold. For many years now I've done everything in my power to be kind and gentle no matter what the situation is. In that moment I got to receive back what I had been giving out to others without any expectations.

After speaking to my client, I knew I also had to address the error with my team and with the specific team member who had been involved in the error. I could have used one of the ineffective and damaging frames that we discussed above and said, "We need to talk!" Or I could have said, "I can't believe you did this!"

Instead of doing that, I chose to create emotional safety for my team member and when we got on the call. The first thing I said was, "The reason I wanted to meet today is because I want to review an error that occurred. I take full responsibility for the error that occurred, and my intention for our time here is both to make sure I understand what happened and also to ensure I give you the support you need so that we can avoid this type of situation in the future."

As we continued our conversation, I let my team member know that while this was a very serious error, I knew that they had not intended to cause any part of it. I also let them know that this error would not be cause for their redeployment (firing) and that all I asked is that they help me create some tools, processes, and policies that would ensure this didn't occur again. I also shared a story with them about a time when I had unintentionally deleted over $50,000 worth of data on a project and how I had learned from that experience.

I also made one request of my team member. I asked them to focus on becoming the best in the world at Google Ads management. I did this because I believe that in times of crisis, we can either beat down those around us or we can empower them and leave lasting positive messaging on their souls.

In that moment both my team member and I knew how serious the situation was. I could see their eyes tearing up, and I continued to let them know that I was in their corner and that this did not have to be a negative experience. Instead I let them know that I believed in them and that I knew they had the potential to become the best in the world at their craft.

During that conversation, I was still managing my own emotions and fighting the urge to be reactive. Now that I look back on the situation, I can tell you that it was one of my proudest moments as a leader and entrepreneur.

Not only did I meet privately with that team member, but I also met with their manager and other team members who were involved at some level. We practiced our guiding principle of positive confrontation along with another one of our guiding principles, which is continuous improvement.

A few days later, after we'd started the path to recovering from that error, one of the team members that was involved shared something really powerful with the entire team on our daily standup.

They said, "You are the kind of boss that I want to follow, Gabe. This week when everything went wrong, you stayed calm. Even in the eye of the storm you were kind, patient, and humble. No matter where I go in life, I will always have you and your words inside me because of how you handled the situation this week, and I feel incredibly blessed to be part of this team."

As they said those kind words to me in front of my entire team, I choked up and tears came to my eyes.

It was also an incredibly valuable experience because my team knows that I won't react in a toxic manner when things are going badly. They know they can come to me even when it's bad. So despite it being an expensive lesson, it was a very valuable one that I cherish to this day.

The question I have for you is: Do you intentionally create emotional safety for those you are called to lead and serve?

If you haven't done well with this in the past, it's OK. I've failed at this so many times. Now that you know how to create this kind of safety for those around you, I encourage you to apologize for past mistakes you made in this area and set a clear intention to do better in the next storm that arises.

There Are Millions of Frames

I've just scratched the surface of the frames that are out there. The key to remember is that you need to be intentional with the frames you set.

When we forget to or choose not to architect a conversation, that means that we often leave the outcome to chance. No wise builder would bring all the tradesmen, materials, and machinery to a job site and then say, "Have at it, everyone! Just build something!"

All great buildings have a blueprint. They have a plan. They aren't left to chance.

I would suggest that you use the same thought process when crafting your important conversations. Yes, there are free-flowing collaboration conversations and open conversations between friends and loved ones, but even those types of conversations can be framed.

If you need to brainstorm or braindump, you can still serve your audience well by framing the conversation effectively for them. Imagine sitting down and saying something like this:

"I haven't structured my thoughts here, so if you're open to it, I'd like to just brainstorm and share what comes to mind. My intention is to share openly and honestly. I want you to know that what we discuss isn't going to be set in stone. I just want to speak freely to start, and then we can bring some definition to the real plan later or in a follow-up conversation."

That frame lets your audience know that you're not sure what you're doing yet and that you just need a sounding board.

Putting it into practice:

You get to create and control the frames you use. I'd encourage you to choose one of the effective frames I shared in this chapter and use it right away today or this week.

Once you've done that, go through the following exercise:

- Write down one frame you experienced that was positive.

- Write down one frame you experienced that was negative.
- Write down one idea of how you can frame a challenging or important conversation for good.

Using frames is a wonderful way to serve your audience, so I would suggest you do it right away!

In the bonuses for the book, I talk about how when I didn't recognize an ineffective frame from another person, I made a terrible choice that destroyed our relationship. If you want to learn how to recognize ineffective frames from others so you can redirect the conversation in a positive manner, check out the bonus resources here: https://atomicwords.com/resources or just scan the QR code below:

CHAPTER 6

SPARC is How You Serve Effective Feedback

"We all need people who will give us feedback. That's how we improve."
— Bill Gates

One of my dear friends, Annabelle Beckwith, the founder of Yara Journeys and author of *Get Your Peas in a Row*, was one of the first leaders in my life to kindly point out to me that using a very common approach called a feedback sandwich is actually very ineffective.

You may have either heard of or experienced this approach before. The theory goes that if you say something nice first, then you'll have your listener warmed up so you can give them the critical feedback that you actually want to share. And then you can wrap it up with something positive as well.

I've actually tried this approach before, and it's ineffective because when you use it, you'll almost always end up eroding trust in the relationship. The reason that it fails is because if you give feedback consistently (as you should regardless of your role on a team), people will start to distrust your positive feedback because it's often followed by some critical feedback.

I'm so glad Annabelle pointed this out to me because it helped me identify a really big gap in my leadership approach. No wonder people didn't believe my compliments. Even though I was truly trying to be sincere in my compliments, the context of how they were delivered made the positivity feel fake at best.

When Annabelle first shared this with me, it put me into a state of contemplation, and I started giving less feedback. Looking back, I realize that this was not an effective decision, but in the moment, I was concerned that I was giving feedback in a way that left a bad taste in peoples' mouths and that's the last thing I ever want to do.

About a year or so after Annabelle pointed that out to me, I was listening to my friend Alex Charfen speak, and he shared two things:

The first was that he required his team to read a book called *Radical Candor*.

The second was that he said he focused on giving very specific feedback, whether it was positive or critical feedback.

Those statements really hit home for me, so I immediately bought the book *Radical Candor* and listened to it. After digging deep into the book, I created a simple tool that my team and I now use on a consistent basis.

It's called SPARC.

At this point, you've probably realized that my tools aren't necessarily spelled right, and that they aren't perfect, but they are effective tools. I can tell you with certainty that ever since we've implemented this tool on our team, we've grown substantially.

One of the most amazing parts of this tool is that I now get consistent feedback back from my team too! If you're an entrepreneur and leader like I am, then you may have noticed that getting feedback from others becomes increasingly harder the more your organization grows.

What I love about this tool is that it gives people around you the freedom and the vehicle with which to serve you and others with highly specific and valuable feedback about their performance and their results.

So what does SPARC stand for? It stands for:

Specific
Praise
And
Really Specific
Candor

When we use SPARC, we truly ignite the situation in a positive manner. We give people actionable feedback that allows them to grow and change. I'd encourage you to write this down now so you can use this focused approach in the future. Giving feedback is one of the most important jobs that any leader and entrepreneur has, so constantly improving your ability to provide feedback is a wise investment in my experience.

As I think about the feedback that I've given and received over the years, I realize that there have been many times the feedback was less than effective.

I remember one time, back when I was working in construction, when I received useless feedback. I was pouring concrete in a driveway and using a tool that is called a straight edge to level it out. My mentor (who was one of the best concrete finishers I ever met) walked up behind me and said, "Get out the way."

I did get out of the way, and he simply grabbed the straight-edge, walked through all my hard work, and redid the work for me. There wasn't any productive feedback outside of me watching him do it the right way. Obviously, having someone set a good example is valuable, but imagine what it would have been like if he also used the SPARC framework.

He could have shared something along these lines with me:

"Gabe, the expectations and standards here are that you keep the concrete perfectly level from one form to the other. Your

actions of not completing the job correctly could have a huge impact on our business and the customer's finished product.

"What's your perspective on this, Gabe? Do you see what I'm pointing out here?

"In the future, I would recommend that you start using the straightedge when the concrete isn't so dried out because it will be easier for you to reach our standards.

"What I'd like to do as a follow-up action is to have you do the second half of the driveway pour today and I'll give you input and help as we go.

"I can see you're trying hard on this and so I want to support you in learning how to do it correctly."

If this approach had been taken with me, I'm certain that I would have learned more effectively and at a much more rapid pace. You can also see in my fictitious example that my mentor did end on a positive note. So to be clear, sandwiching constructive criticism and feedback between two positive statements is generally ineffective. However, I do believe it's wise to end on a positive note whenever possible.

There are some additional keys to providing effective feedback that truly serves your audience.

Remember to use an effective frame.

In almost *all cases* I choose to start with an intention statement along these lines:

"Hi, Charlie. My intention with our time today is to serve you and share what I'm seeing as it relates to your performance on the implementation team."

Don't leave your intentions behind, but instead make them clear up front. This will, in my personal experience, align your attitude and heart in the right direction so you can actually deliver effective and kind feedback.

For positive feedback, feel free to do so in a group.

When you start to implement this new feedback framework, I believe it's wise to intentionally balance your positive and critical feedback. If you only tell someone when they're doing something wrong, they'll be left guessing as to when they are doing things right.

So when someone does a great job, make a habit of pointing that out in a group setting. Praise them honestly and stick to the positive part of the feedback.

For constructive criticism, start by doing so in private.

With very sensitive topics or when you have to address something more negative, deliver that feedback in a private meeting. This approach typically allows your ego and the other person's ego to get in the way less. You can also address your concerns more candidly in this format.

Be sure to use SPARC and also utilize the recommendations that my friend Annabelle speaks about in her book.

- Share the expectations and standards you have for them.
- Let them know what actions you're giving feedback on and what impact those actions had.
- Get their perspective, as this will often shed light on the best solutions for the future.
- Remember to outline what you expect them to do differently in the future.
- Create a follow-up plan before ending your meeting so you're both clear on the next checkpoint.

This approach of delivering the more difficult feedback and constructive criticism should be practiced for a while along with positive feedback so that you can move to the next type of feedback we'll cover.

While I believe that each situation and audience is different, as a general rule of thumb I like to ask my coaching clients to practice these first two forms of feedback for at least 90 days. Ensure that each person in your audience (clients and team members) get used to receiving positive feedback in private and in a group setting, and also constructive feedback one on one.

I don't remember which of my friends shared this with me, but I heard once (and now subscribe to this belief) that every time you give candid and critical feedback, you should have already given that team member five positive bits of feedback. When I heard that, it made a lot of sense to me. If I chose to only share critical feedback with my team, then eventually they would begin to believe that all they did was mess up. Continued negative messaging may either break their spirit, hurt their feelings, or eventually drive them out of the company.

As leaders our job is to nurture all of those around us like a master gardener. We need to tend to those in our garden with love, sunlight, water, and gentle adjustment. Yes, here and there we may need to trim something off or do something slightly more drastic, but that can't be the majority of our work.

I remember on one occasion in my company Business Marketing Engine when a new team member had just recently joined our Search Engine Optimization (SEO) team a few months prior. We had asked them to join our team so they could focus on getting high domain rank links back to our clients' sites. This is a very important part of SEO because it's what tells Google that a site is credible and worth sending traffic to.

I'm going to expound upon the link-building work for two reasons. First, because it will help you understand how I used specific praise to serve my team members well, and second, because I believe that all entrepreneurs in our era need to understand how SEO works. If you don't understand the principles behind SEO, then you may run into trouble. You'll either miss out on valuable traffic that will turn into revenue for your business, or in a worst case you may have an inexperienced or dishonest SEO company mislead you on what they are actually doing.

After I shared this analogy with a client of ours, I asked one of my copywriters, to watch the video and write it out.

How do you improve a website's domain rating?

Imagine it this way: Jim and Sharon are competitors selling the same product, and they've both been invited to speak on a panel at a conference to explain the benefits of their products. There are about a thousand people attending this conference, and just as many businesses there too.

Jim shows up at the conference an hour before it's time for him to speak at the panel. He's making personal connections with people, handing out his business cards, introducing himself and explaining how his product can help them. Sharon, on the other hand, shows up right on time, just before both she and Jim go on stage to speak at the panel.

The emcee of the panel introduces Jim and Sharon, and then they dive into their presentations. Both Jim and Sharon explain their product's features, answer audience questions, and share their expertise. All in all, the panel goes well, with Jim and Sharon getting fairly equal speaking time.

But, here comes the twist.

At the end of the panel, the emcee decides to poll the audience, asking which of the two presenters they think is more credible (the answer ultimately deciding who they'll buy a product from).

With everything you've read so far, who do you think the audience will point to?

They would point to Jim.

Even though Jim and Sharon had the same stage time and did well during the panel, Sharon didn't go out and make individual connections to build credibility. Jim made those connections, building credibility before he even started speaking at the panel.

And **that's how Google works with domain ratings**. Domain ratings are based on how many other high-domain rating credible sites link back to a website, or, using our analogy, how many connections Jim made before the panel started.

Think about a really old established website. They have a domain rating of 95 –100 because they've been around for so long and people link to them all the time. If they backlink to a website, Google sees that site as a more credible source.

So, to increase a client's website's domain rating, we go out and look for other credible sources to cite and link to our client's webpage, showing that they are the best option to pick for service. Continuing to do that over time increases their web traffic because the more other sites reference them, the more it increases their credibility.

That's the story that we share with our clients when we explain how we're going to increase their websites' domain rankings and bring them more traffic.

The newer team member I mentioned earlier was effectively reaching out to get some links for our client's site, but as I reviewed her work, I realized that she wasn't getting them fast enough. Instead of choosing to focus on the negative, I actually turned it around. I shared with her how pleased I was with her link building efforts, and I asked her to focus on getting more links in a shorter period of time. She was not only pleased to receive that encouragement, but she was able to start moving more quickly in her work as well.

The result of my feedback to her was that in about 11 months, we took our client's website from a domain ranking of 8 all the way to 46. Because of that our client had an 802% increase in traffic compared to six months earlier! Now our client is consistently seeing a 65% month over month increase in traffic, and they are quickly becoming a market leader in their space.

That's just one example of the power of providing specific praise when you give feedback. I would encourage you to pause here and take note of the areas where you can give specific praise to your team and your clients. In my opinion, everyone in our lives deserves to receive praise when they do a job well. This approach will give those around you the rocket fuel they need to grow more quickly. They will be able to provide better results for you and your clients.

Anecdotal Constructive Feedback in a Group Setting:

Another one of the most valuable types of feedback that I've implemented with my team is anecdotal feedback in group settings. In my experience, this should only be implemented after you're confident that you have a high degree of trust in your organization or on your team.

One of my longest time mentors and friends, Doug Beaver, first introduced me to this approach, and it has been incredibly effective over the years. In order to begin using this method with your team, I recommend approaching it in the following manner:

1. Begin by watching for a situation where you personally made a mistake that should be addressed.

2. Write some notes down on how you would provide feedback to someone who made this mistake (imagining it wasn't you).

3. In your next team meeting, open up with a statement along these lines (in your own words, of course):

"Team, one of the things that I believe will help us move forward and grow is to provide anecdotal feedback and constructive criticism during our team meetings.

"As an example, I want to share with you how I really dropped the ball and failed on the XYZ project.

*"As you know, our **standard** is to send a project update email at the end of each week. I failed to do that **(your own actions)** and because of it the project was delayed **(impact of your actions)**.*

*"My perspective on why this happened is that I overbooked myself on Friday and completely forgot to do what is required. **(This outlines the "their perspective" part of the feedback framework)**.*

*"In the **future** I'm going to block out time at the end of the day Friday to ensure I complete my project updates.*

*"Additionally, I'd like to ask you, Christian, to check back with me in two weeks to see how this new plan is working. **(The follow-up plan)**.*

"I think it would be wise for all of us to consider blocking time in our calendars for these kinds of priorities."

That's how you introduce constructive criticism in a group setting.

In your next team get-together, you can then say:

"Remember how last time I shared how I dropped the ball, and I used the situation to share how I plan to improve and how we can all improve?"

Explain to them how you gave yourself feedback and that with the intention of serving each of them and helping the whole team grow, you will be sharing some anecdotal feedback in the group setting going forward.

In my opinion these are some best practices for giving feedback in group settings:

- Always approach it with kindness and respect.
- State your intentions of service and love up front. If you're not coming from that place in your heart, don't do it.
- Keep it pretty light to start.
- Don't tackle deep issues until you've really established trust in the group.
- Confront situations where one person's actions have impacted others and the feedback and solution needs to be a group effort.
- Take full ownership of the feedback.
- Don't say "I heard someone say…"
- Stick to the feedback you have for them personally.
- Be open to their perspective and input as well.

While there is no perfect formula for giving feedback, I do have total confidence that this framework will guide you in the right direction. This is because when I implemented this into our daily huddle with the team, I saw the team really enjoyed receiving consistent and clear feedback.

I also believe that when you approach each feedback session with the intention of serving your audience and helping them grow, then you can be kind and respectful, regardless of how tough the subject matter is.

The other advantage of giving yourself feedback in this manner is that over time, your team will be more comfortable with providing you feedback. You will still need to ask them for feedback on a consistent basis, but if you keep at it, you'll start to get some of the other leaders on your team to give you that feedback. In my experience, it's often difficult to get your team to provide you with feedback because they were most likely shot down by previous leaders they tried to give feedback to. Or worst case, I've heard of team members being fired for speaking up. Hearing things like that always makes me sick, but I've learned that I essentially have to rehabilitate new team members and let them know that they are completely safe to share any and all feedback they have in a respectful manner.

With time, coaching, and coaxing, I've been able to get many of my team members to give me feedback on my own performance and ideas. It's truly a gift when you are able to get those around you to give you feedback, so keep asking until you get it!

Most importantly, start using SPARC right away.

One of my personal values in life and business is positive confrontation. I've confronted many different things over the years. While it never feels super comfortable to confront someone and give them constructive criticism, in almost all cases it leads to a positive outcome.

I believe that you cannot become an effective communicator unless you learn to consistently confront people and provide healthy feedback.

Putting it into practice:

Think about someone who needs your service and support. Someone who needs feedback on the positive side of things and also someone who needs constructive criticism. Take time to write out your plan on how you intend to confront them in a positive manner and provide valuable feedback. If you're really uncomfortable at first, that's OK. Start with some simple, smaller points of feedback, and work up to the big issues that you've been avoiding.

Be patient with yourself, and remember to always state your intentions up front. As you begin to practice this feedback framework, take time to set a goal of how often you should give positive and constructive feedback each month.

This is a critical habit and skill that will take your entrepreneurial communication skills to the next level, so be sure to intentionally practice these skills!

One of the things that surprised me the most about SPARC was how my team started using it quickly after I introduced it to them. In the bonuses for this book, I share a podcast episode where one of my team members, Becca, used SPARC to help me change and grow the company.

What is so exciting about using SPARC consistently is that you as the entrepreneur and leader will have the opportunity to get more consistent feedback for yourself. If you coach your team and truly ask from your heart for feedback, over time, they will often give it to you. And then you've established mutual trust and respect, which is the glue of successful team cultures.

Check out the SPARC section in the bonuses here: https://atomicwords.com/resources or just scan the QR code below:

CHAPTER 7

Solid Anchors

"While scuba diving off the British Virgin Islands about 25 years ago, our boat's anchor got stuck. I dived down to release it, but I got separated from the boat and was stranded as it sped away. I had to swim for an hour to the nearest island with all my scuba kit on before I was rescued."
— Sir David Jason

Have you ever stood next to a large cruise ship, or seen a picture of one? I remember when I got off a Disney cruise ship a few years back. We had just docked at a port in Italy, and I was walking down the long dock towards the town where we stopped.

On the opposite side of the dock, another cruise ship was in the process of docking, and the ship dropped a giant 20-ton anchor into the harbor. There was a huge splash, and the clanking of the chain as it ran out the side of the ship was deafening for a moment.

Cruise ships can weigh approximately 200,000 tons, and it always amazes me how an anchor that is only one ten thousandth of the ship's weight can hold it down so well. Granted, large cruise ships can have between two and four anchors, but still, even at 80 tons total for all four anchors, that's only four ten thousandths of the weight of the ship.

It's crazy to observe, and it's also a great analogy as it relates to how we anchor things in our communication. According to "the Google," the average sentence has around 20 words in it, and the average human who is speaking for five minutes speaks around 750 words. That's where the magic of anchors comes into play.

As entrepreneurs and leaders I believe that we need to place a higher value, and higher intention, on how and what we anchor to in our communication. Imagine your partner comes into the room right now and says, *"We have a massive fire to handle right now!"*

Because our brains tend to analyze everything based on the initial anchor that we hear first in a conversation, your mind (and body in most cases too) would instantly be put on high alert after your partner said that first sentence to you. Everything that came after that sentence would be anchored to the fact that you were told that *"We have a massive fire to handle…"*

That's a somewhat dramatic example, but if it's used with intention and care, it could be freeing by the fact that your partner has let you know the severity of the situation before even getting into all the context of what's going on.

Similarly, we can anchor conversations, copy, videos, and really any type of written or verbal communication with positive anchors that can be just as freeing. Now imagine that your partner walks into the room right now and says, *"What I'm about to tell you may feel overwhelming at first, but I want you to know that I'm already handling it and things are going to be fine."*

That approach may instead anchor you to a feeling that this is important, but that your partner is already handling it and that you don't have to worry about anything serious. How we anchor our messaging, our conversations, and all of our communication is an often overlooked but an incredibly important and freeing principle of communication.

I opened this chapter with the quote from Sir David Jason because I believe that without proper anchors in our communication, we are essentially leaving our audience to fend for themselves in the rough tides of unclear communication. If we aren't intentionally anchoring our conversations, then we're leaving our audience to "die" in the sea of context, or they may have to "swim" for hours to understand what was really said.

Anchors are a highly effective communication tool that can be used with multiple different audiences. Whether you're selling to someone, or simply trying to teach a new concept, you can anchor on a concept, a price point, or any other anchor that will help you serve your audience.

My good friend Jay Crouch was on a call with me a few months back and used a great anchor to help explain a very technical concept. Instead of trying to explain the exact algorithm that was needed to perform the amazing software functions that occur in blockchain technology, he simply equated the concept to depositing money with a bank teller.

That allowed me to start constructing my ideas, the data he was sharing, and other concepts around an anchor I already understood. In this case the anchor was an analogy that served us both well because we could refer back to some common ground. In other cases we use anchors to affix someone's focus on something so that they get a better perspective on what we're sharing.

Price Anchors

A few years ago, right after my partner Rachel and I had purchased our house, we decided to stop at a billiards store while we were out shopping. The previous owners had left the pool table in the basement, and the table was in good shape. Unfortunately, the pool queues that were left weren't straight, and their tips were completely worn out or broken off.

So when I walked into the store, the owner met me and started showing me all the different options available. He had owned the store for decades and was truly passionate about what he sold. As we started walking around the showroom, he began by showing me a pool stick that cost $1,500.

As we progressed through all the options, he showed me his lowest-end sticks, which were $40 to $90 each. When I walked out of the store that day, I had a pool stick that cost me $600 and had a lifetime warranty. If I'm really honest with myself, it doesn't improve my game much, but what I did enjoy as part of my buying experience was choosing something that felt high value but that wasn't the most expensive option.

Most buyers operate this way.

That's why if you want to create a pleasant experience without negative pressure for your prospects, you should always sell "top down" by anchoring on the highest price option and then sharing the progressively lower priced options. Most buyers will land in the middle somewhere, just like I did.

This simple anchoring technique works flawlessly, and it allows the prospect to self select into the right option. When they make the choice to buy at the level they want, then they are far less likely to have complaints or ask for a refund. Choice is important, and in order to help people make the right choice, it's our responsibility to anchor correctly on what matters.

Emotional Anchors

Right now I want you to imagine that you just received a terrible phone call from the hospital. A friend of yours was in a car accident. They are OK overall, but it's going to be a few weeks before they are fully recovered.

Now imagine that you spilled your coffee or tea on the floor and had to stop what you were doing and clean it up. Which incident are you most upset about? I would guess that you're not upset at all about spilling your drink.

You may be emotional about it because of the bad news about your friend, but in reality, you probably wouldn't give much thought to the spilled drink in comparison to the bad news the hospital delivered to you.

While that is an example of negative emotional anchoring, you can use a positive anchor too. Now imagine you are at your favorite vacation spot with your loved ones. You're relaxing and enjoying your time off without a care in the world.

You just got a call that one of your businesses sold and now you have tens of millions of dollars free and clear in your personal bank accounts. There is nothing to worry about at all because you and your loved ones are happy, healthy, and wealthy.

In that moment, what possibilities would you start exploring for your future? Would you start a charity? Would you buy or start another business?

Since I anchored your thoughts on an incredibly positive situation, and helped open your imagination up, you now have the brain space to dream. That's what's so powerful about anchors.

One of the simplest and shortest anchors I use on a regular basis has helped me in so many different ways as an entrepreneur. I want to share it with you.

"If you could wave a magic wand and change anything in your business, what would you change?"

That simple anchor has helped me serve my clients by helping them imagine what is truly possible. It's helped me close more deals because I then know exactly what people are struggling with.

Learning how to strategically use anchors is very helpful. I believe that there are many anchors that should be rooted in imagination. The reason I believe this is because my good friend Ryan Chute said something powerful to me one day. He said, "No one can do *anything at all* until they imagine themselves doing it."

That statement really stuck with me, and it helped me understand that we need to serve our audience by opening up their imagination. For me there is another interesting facet of this concept. Manifestation is something that may be on the edge of being too "woo woo" for you and is often taught in spiritual circles. It's something that I personally believe in though, and I honestly believe in it more from a practical and mental standpoint.

If someone wants more income, they first have to imagine making more. Whatever mechanism they use to do that, either selling more, climbing the corporate ladder, or creating value in other forms, they still have to imagine themselves doing that.

Knowing that imagination is the key that unlocks our unlimited potential is a principle that I would strongly recommend you explore. It is useful for both your own internal goals and also for the audiences you speak to.

I'll give you an example of how I used the magic wand anchor to help one of our clients unlock their entrepreneurial dreams.

When I met with my friend and client Edwin Wu, I asked him that question, and he started to share his dream of how he wanted to serve those with type 2 diabetes. Since Edwin is an emergency care physician, he has experienced what the traditional medical system is like and how it doesn't always provide the best patient experience. He is confident that he can provide a better patient care experience to those with this disease. We spent a few meetings working out his vision, and then my team and I went to work.

We created an 18-month plan that we presented to Edwin a month later. Inside the plan we showed him how we could help him effortlessly write a book as the first part of his offer. We shared with him how that book would be the first touch point in his customer journey that would ultimately lead to his customers joining his private paid community.

Inside the plan we presented we gave him a detailed blueprint of how we'd build his web and mobile app that would allow him to serve many customers with this disease and also generate revenue for his business.

From the front side offer, to designing his logo, website, mobile app, email marketing, and many other elements of his business, we were able to clearly present a plan to him that all originated from me asking him that magic wand question that anchored him in the right place.

By the time this book is released, our team will have already built out the majority of his technology and marketing, and he will be well on his way to having a successful and profitable business. Projects like that are some of my favorite ones to partner with our clients on, and they all begin with a simple anchor.

You can use contrasting or negative imaginative anchors as well.

In order to help someone consider their risks, here's an anchor that could be used (if framed well with a true intention of service before opening this part of your conversation up). Here's how you could anchor for a positive outcome with a negative anchor:

Imagine that you wake up tomorrow and find out your general manager was stealing thousands of dollars from you every month.

How would you react?

What measures would you put in place to prevent this in the future?

How would you design your systems so that they are more transparent and eliminate as much temptation as possible for future team members?

That's an example of how you can use a potentially negative idea to help someone make positive changes.

How to Use Extremes for You and Your Audience's Benefit

One of the best anchors I use is when I explore the extreme edges of a scenario. If I truly sit down and imagine what the extremes would look like, I'm able to make a better decision.

Sometimes I like to ask my audience this question:

"What is the absolute worst-case scenario that could happen if nothing goes right and everything goes wrong?"

We discuss or write down the answers, and I really push them hard to see what is possible.

Then I ask the other question:

"What is the absolute best-case scenario that could happen if literally every part of this plan goes incredibly well?"

We then write down or discuss those options.

After going through that exercise, it's fairly simple to create a realistic scenario based on the two extremes. This is because oftentimes the middle of the road is where things generally land.

Thinking about an extreme case (even if you don't use the opposite extreme) can help you and your audience imagine a very different scenario. You can anchor on one point for leverage and then make progress and decisions based on that viewpoint.

What's important to remember is that you can influence behavior in a significant way when you strategically choose the right anchor point.

As you consider the past few major decisions you made, you may discover that you were anchored on a particular price, emotion, or imaginary state. Reviewing how you received that anchor is valuable as well.

Not only should we learn how to serve our audience with the proper use of anchors; we should also become more aware of our own self-imposed anchors. We can also explore how others around us are anchoring us to something so we can evaluate their motives and see if their intentions are to serve and help us, or to manipulate us in a negative way.

Moving your own anchors:

Earlier today, before sitting down to complete this chapter, I was reflecting on my business. I had just received a cancellation notice from a client. I was disappointed because they had mismanaged their time and funds, stopped focusing on their sales efforts, and had never made a solid effort to follow up on the hundreds of leads we had generated for them.

In that moment I found myself getting anchored on that negative feeling that somehow we had failed (even though the data told a different story). I never want to see a client fail, even if we've done everything in our power to help them succeed. I was feeling discouraged about it, but not only did the data from the client's campaign show that we had been successful, but the impact to my business was also incredibly small. That client canceling removed less than 1% of our operating revenue, and so it didn't really logically make sense that I was feeling upset about it, but in my experience, emotions aren't always logical.

What I decided to do in that moment is use a tool that I learned from a self-therapy app called Bloom. The tool is called Catch, Challenge, Change. When you have a thought that doesn't serve you well, you can notice that anchor and catch it. Then you can challenge the emotional anchor and change it if you want to.

I decided to Catch, Challenge, and Change from that anchor to a positive one. Just a few days before the small cancellation came in, we signed a deal worth nearly 20% of our revenue. In that moment I decided to refocus and anchor on the amazing success we've been having instead of staying stuck on the negative anchor.

While that is an example of how to speak to yourself and move anchors, the same thing applies when you're speaking to an audience beyond yourself. We have the power to choose, change, and update the anchors we are using in our communications. Don't ever underestimate the power of having the right anchor in place.

Putting it into practice:

Think about the last time you had a conversation that held your attention for a long time.

What emotion or deep desire did they anchor on?

How can you anchor your audience on something that will help them grow? How can you serve them with a strong anchor?

On the sales front, if you've never explored price anchoring before, then I have good news for you. In the bonus section about anchors, I have a short training video about pricing anchors and how they can help you. If you don't already have the bonuses, grab them here: https://atomicwords.com/resources or just scan the QR code below:

CHAPTER 8

Emotional Labeling

"Gratitude is the healthiest of all human emotions. The more you express gratitude for what you have, the more likely you will have even more to express gratitude for."
— Zig Ziglar

I remember when I first sat down to watch Mike Birbiglia perform his stand-up comedy feature on Netflix called "My Girlfriend's Boyfriend." My partner, Rachel, and I watched it one night, and it left a lasting impression.

Mike describes how he met his girlfriend (who became his wife) and how baffled he was by the fact that his girlfriend didn't really have logical reasons for everything she said and did. At the end of the stand-up he uses one line as he's sharing what his girlfriend said after an argument they had. All she said to justify her position in their argument (as I remember it) was, "Well, that's just how I feel."

I remember realizing in that moment that feelings are powerful and that when we choose to acknowledge and label them, we have the opportunity to communicate more clearly and serve others in a much better way. One of the most powerful pieces of acknowledging feelings is that they are always valid. Mike Birbiglia realizes that there's really nothing he can say to refute his girlfriend. It's just how she feels.

The same applies to all of us, men, women, and children. All humans have that same condition. We can't necessarily logically prove our feelings; we just feel the way we feel. Our feelings change. I believe that emotion is a powerful tool to have on our side, and I do not believe that it's wise to push our emotions down or ask anyone around you to ignore their feelings.

It is very important, powerful, and healthy (both on the individual and organizational level) to acknowledge and label our feelings. The great part of realizing and labeling your feelings is that it will help you release some tension and it will help your audience empathize with where you're at.

Just like Zig Ziglar labeled the feeling of gratitude and its positive result, we can label all our emotions in a manner that allows us to identify them and manage them in a healthy way.

If I come into your office today and say, "I'm really mad at you!" then you'll be anchored to a position that may not serve us well if we're trying to productively work together. What would be more effective would be for me to approach the conversation this way:

"I want you to know that my intention is to serve you and help us both move forward. Because of that I want to share some honest and respectful thoughts with you. Right now <u>I feel very frustrated</u> and upset about the way that the last meeting we had together ended. I feel like I wasn't being listened to, so I ended up just shutting down and not sharing openly. I'd like to find a way to work together on this project and I felt it was important to share my honest feelings."

When we start with "I feel" statements, we are honoring the truth of our own emotions and not coming from a place of judgment. If I start the conversation in an accusatory manner, then you will automatically be on the defense and our free flowing transfer of information will be restricted or shut down.

When I'm simply presenting my feelings, that gives you (my audience) the chance to respond empathetically. Obviously, not everyone will respond with empathy, and so we have to realize that we need to set boundaries on what we will accept behavior wise from others. This is important because we can set the standard that we will not tolerate someone cursing at us or bullying us.

Those are important boundaries to identify personally; however, in my experience, I've rarely seen anyone respond poorly to sincere "I feel" statements. When you approach someone with kindness and honesty and you sincerely share how you're feeling, then you are setting the stage for healthy communication.

As entrepreneurs we don't always realize that others aren't in our heads. They can't see how we feel or how we're processing what happens in the world around us. I didn't realize how limited my emotional labeling language was until a friend of mine shared this Emotion Wheel chart with me:

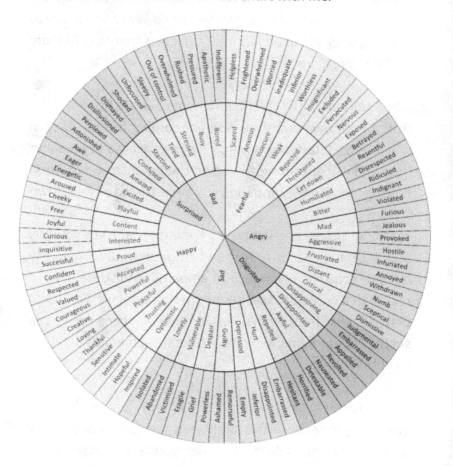

After I studied the chart, I realized that I don't think I've ever said, "I feel powerless" or "I feel dismayed right now."

Despite the fact that we have an incredibly powerful set of descriptors for our emotions, we don't always utilize them effectively. I also believe that in many cases, entrepreneurs had very different upbringings and weren't taught the full spectrum of emotional language.

One of my goals after just beginning to explore this area of my personal development is to model healthy emotional language to my son. I grew up in a home where there was nearly zero positive communication between my parents and there was absolutely no "I feel" statement modeling. There *was* a lot of giving the silent treatment or screaming every few months when things built up to a breaking point.

Learning to label your emotions will not only help you serve your audience in a much more effective manner, but it will help you discover more about yourself. I believe that it's very important to realize that the more you get to know yourself, love yourself, and accept how you operate naturally, the more you can impact the world around you.

While I'm not religious anymore, I did read the Bible a few times cover to cover, and one of the verses that always stood out to me says, "Before you point out the speck in your brother's eye, be sure to remove the plank from your own eye!"

I think what the writer was getting at is that if we really want to help others, we first need to make sure that we have helped ourselves by being healthy and whole. Personal development takes many different forms, and it's hard work. Even though it can be incredibly difficult to do the internal work necessary, the outcomes are always worth it. When we solve our own hurts, shortcomings, and lack of vocabulary (emotional or otherwise), we begin to unlock deeper meaning and more effective leverage points.

If you think about one of the times you were most hurt by someone else, it was probably because they were having a difficult emotional time and they lashed out at you.

How did that make you feel?

Often when people are hurting emotionally, they blame us for things or speak irrationally. Instead of using clear vocabulary and saying, "I feel angry that this happened," it's normal for people to say, "I'm so angry at you!" When you recognize this in others, you can begin to develop the skill of using emotional labeling yourself.

One thing that I like to practice, and I encourage you to practice, is pausing when you feel triggered. In those moments when someone is reacting emotionally instead of taking time to respond responsibly, it's very easy to allow the emotions we feel to drag us into a different state of mind and different emotional state.

Recently, I was discussing an upcoming expense with a partner of mine. We hadn't planned for a $2,500 bill that came in, and my partner responded by saying how unfair it was that we had to take that out of the project budget. I could see that this unexpected expense had triggered something in them and in my head, I agreed that it wasn't fair.

On a scale of 1 – 10 their emotional response was probably a 6 or 7, and I could tell that they were angry. In the past I would have become very invested in trying to make them understand why it happened, or I would have agreed with them and matched their level of emotionality in the moment. Neither of those reactions would have changed the fact that this unexpected expense came up.

Instead of doing what I used to, I replied that I understood how they felt. I validated their feelings, and I also reminded them that even though it wasn't fair, we could absorb the overage in the project and still be OK overall. I didn't react, but instead responded. Within a matter of minutes, my partner came back to me and said, "I'm OK. Everything is fine, and I'm not actually that worried about that expense." I was proud of both of us in that moment for two reasons: first, I didn't react and match the level of emotions that my partner was feeling. Second, we both had a high enough level of self-awareness to respond and also quickly adjust after the initial situation.

By modeling this kind of behavior to those around you, and by becoming more versed in labeling the emotions that you feel, you can efficiently navigate the many emotions that we feel and encounter on a daily basis.

Putting it into practice:

Replay a conversation you had that turned negative. Was there a point that you could have used an "I am feeling like" label to share honestly without raising tension?

Write down a better approach for the conversation so you can utilize it next time.

Additionally, take a moment to review the emotions chart shared earlier in the chapter and ask yourself if you can be more specific next time you label the emotions you're feeling.

In the bonuses for this book, I have a section where I share how I use emotional labeling on a daily basis to create more momentum in my personal life and business. Be sure to check it out here: https://atomicwords.com/resources or just scan the QR code below:

THE MINDSET

In order for us to communicate effectively as entrepreneurs, we need to have the right mindset around communication and decision making. While we've definitely touched on some of the mindsets around effective communication in earlier chapters, this section will take a deeper dive into powerful mindsets that you can adopt around your communication.

As we approach each new conversation with a single audience member or with larger groups, I believe that it's key to have done the internal mindset work ahead of time whenever possible. This allows us to come to the conversations we have in a prepared manner.

When we know what we think, how we should deliver our communication, and we know why we're doing it, then the opportunity for positive and effective communication increases dramatically.

While not every aspect of these mindset tools I'm going to share are 100% about communication, they do, in my experience, support the kind of communication that you need in order to be successful as an entrepreneur and leader.

As you go through this final section of the book, I'd encourage you to not only be open to these mindset tools and strategies, but I'd also ask you to think about other mindsets that you may need to adopt in order to become more effective in your communication. Personally, I've found that when I choose to be open to the possibility that I need to improve my own mindset, I discover more powerful mindset shifts that I can make.

As I shared earlier in the book, my friend Ryan Chute said, "No one can do *anything at all* until they imagine themselves doing it." That same principle applies here. If you can imagine the possibility that you may need to improve your mindset, and you start to imagine that there are new mindset tools that can help you, then they will start to show themselves to you.

My encouragement to you today as you're reading this is to choose to be as open minded as possible so that you can have a more powerful and effective mindset.

So with that said, let's dive into the next chapter.

CHAPTER 9

The Circle of Life

"Waiting hurts. Forgetting hurts. But not knowing which decision to take can sometimes be the most painful..."
— José N. Harris

I remember when my client Jody first called me. She was overwhelmed with her technology problems. She was underwhelmed with her marketing efforts. Even though she'd been growing a team for a few years, and had nearly two dozen employees, she was still the primary decision maker.

When something went wrong, Jody's team came to her. When there was a new opportunity, again, her team came to her to ask permission. As the business grew, Jody found herself working longer hours and getting less and less done.

That was until I introduced The Circle of Life decision making process to her and her team. In just a couple hours we sat down and walked her entire team through this simple exercise.

And in just a few days, the entire team was talking about and implementing The Circle of Life.

The Circle of Life contains just a few words that help leaders and entrepreneurs harness the power of their entire team's creative brain power. It helps remove the bottleneck that is often unintentionally created as our organizations grow.

I remember when I first discovered The Circle of Life decision making and prioritization framework. I had hired my friend Annabelle Beckwith to do some consulting work for me. I didn't realize it at the time, but I was trying to adjust my culture, and Annabelle is brilliant at that kind of work.

While I didn't fully understand exactly what organizational culture was at the time, I now feel like I have a firmer grasp of it. I recently heard a statement that clearly defined culture. As I often do, I chose to expand the definition into my own words so that I would remember it.

Here's the definition I came up with:

"Effective company culture is when you know that your team would make the same decision as you would when they encounter a decision-making point in their role."

Would you honestly say that everyone on your team, and even your vendors would make the same kind of decision as you would? I know I haven't always been able to answer that question with a yes.

I remember when Annabelle and I first got together to meet about this challenge I was facing, I said to her, "I wish I didn't have to make all the decisions in my company!" And in her as always brilliant manner, Annabelle helped me uncover this powerful framework that I designed to help my team make better decisions. While this isn't by any means the be-all, end-all culture tool, it is a great starting place for you and your team.

You don't have to sing Elton John's song "The Circle of Life" to use this tool, but hey, if that helps it stick in your mind, then go for it. I didn't realize that I had named my tool after his song until after the fact, but maybe I was subconsciously going for that effect anyway.

The first question you need to ask yourself in The Circle of Life is: Is this what's best for the company?

The second question you need to ask yourself in The Circle of Life is: Is this what's best for the entire team and individual team members as well?

The third question you need to ask yourself in The Circle of Life is: Is this what's best for our clients?

As I explained this process to my team, they started to understand how their decisions affect others and also how they should be thinking. As an example, if something is what's best for the company and, in fact, hurts the company, then it will lose profits. If that happens, the company could go out of business and leave its team members jobless. If the company and team are no longer there, then the clients will not be served and supported and will suffer and have to go elsewhere.

In contrast, if the decision is made that is best for the company, it can take care of the team. If the team is well taken care of as a whole and on an individual basis, then they can serve the clients at the highest level and do what's best for them. When we truly partner with our clients and do what's best for them, they succeed, have a positive experience, and can keep paying the company which is what's best for the company.

What's absolutely critical is that everyone understands that there is no starting point for the circle of life; it's infinite.

So while the decision-making priority is cascading in some senses, you also could start from any level. The company, team, or client level.

No decision is made at just the company level, just the team level, or just the client level. All three levels are a filtering framework that help us discover the full impact of the choice we are considering.

The framework also helps us realign our focus to where it should be: client service. When we choose to serve our clients at the highest level, we truly have the opportunity to grow an amazing organization.

Money is infinite, but clients are not.

As Don Peppers and Martha Rogers teach in their book *Rules to Break & Laws to Follow: How Your Business Can Beat the Crisis of Short-Termism*, client equity is one of the most important factors to measure in business. If with every interaction with a client you delight them, surprise them in a good way, and increase their trust in you as a person and your organization, then your client value increases.

In Stephen M. R. Covey's book *The Speed of Trust: The One Thing That Changes Everything,* he covers in great depth how trust is one of the most foundational elements of an organization's success. Warren Buffet is a wonderful example of how trust can deliver value at speed. Covey talks about him in his book, and here are a couple of examples of how Warren Buffett chooses to trust.

There are many great books that talk about this, but I want to call out a particular story that stuck with me long after I read it.

In 1983, Buffett bought an 80% interest in Nebraska Furniture Mart on a handshake from the Blumkin family. He said he had often wanted to buy the store, so on his birthday he walked in and wrote them a check for $55 million and shook hands with them.

After reading Buffet's biography *The Snowball*, I discovered that he chose to do business this way whenever possible. He also purchased McLane Distribution (a company with $23 billion in revenue) from Wal-Mart for $1.45 billion (yes, billion with a B) on a handshake. The only way that it was possible to do that was that both parties had complete trust in the other party. I'm sharing these examples because trust truly is one of the most important things you need to focus on in order to fully execute on the circle of life.

For there to be a healthy decision-making progress, your team has to trust that you are making decisions at the company level that are best for the team and the clients. And your clients have to trust that your team is making decisions that are best for them.

Focusing on a true win win win is what makes The Circle of Life work. So as I've said, and to be explicitly clear: you have to filter a decision through all three layers of the circle of life. It's not one or two; it's all three. When you take this approach, you set yourself and your team up for success.

Here are a few examples of how we've implemented The Circle of Life in our company at Business Marketing Engine.

1. The Writer's Guide

Copywriter Today is a content creation and copywriting service that we offer to our clients. We create blog posts, email marketing content, ebooks, and many other forms of content marketing for our clients. One of our editors who supports our writers noticed that some of the orders for content that we were receiving weren't as clear as they ideally should be, so she took initiative and wrote a guide called "How to Improve Your Content." It was designed for the clients and the writers.

It talked about how the clients could provide more specific information to our **company**, so that way our **team** of writers could provide better work. That way the **client** would trust us more and receive an excellent level of service, and keep paying the company.

That is a simple example of how powerful this mindset is and how an infinite amount of value can be created when everyone is in proper alignment with The Circle of Life.

2. Prioritizing Client Requests

Another great example that occurred on our team was when one of my product leaders reached out to cancel a meeting with me. They cancelled because an unexpected client issue had come up, and they decided that it was more important to meet with the client and resolve the issue than it was to keep a lower priority meeting with me. Serving our clients at the highest level means that when they need something we do whatever we can to support them and solve the challenges they are having.

While that type of decision can't be made in a vacuum without considering what's best for the company and team as well, it does make sense to keep a client happy and keep building that trust. That means the client can continue to pay our company, and our team can be paid as well and provide excellent work to the client.

Do you see how The Circle of Life just flows in a never-ending circle?

The key is to remember that this tool needs to be used in a balanced and effective manner. You can't constantly cancel internal operations meetings for clients and actually serve them well because you'll end up with a poor operations team that hurts the company and the client.

So as with all tools, this approach needs to be applied with care and intention so that it's truly being utilized in a wise manner.

Because The Circle of Life is a principle-based framework, as an entrepreneur and leader you can use it as the basis of your one-on-one coaching sessions with those around you as well. Here are a few examples of how I've used it with my team.

In the years leading up to the publication of this book, our team has grown exponentially from 10 – 12 full-time team members to now having over 40 full-time team members. While this growth has been very exciting, successful, and profitable overall, it hasn't come without its share of challenges. One of the challenges that we uncovered and started solving early in our scaling process was that we didn't have effective project-level hours tracking.

We were already using a great time-tracking tool called Hub-staff for payroll purposes, but it really wasn't built in such a way that it meshed with our project management style. When we realized this challenge, we started adding additional tools. First, we started out by tracking things in a Google Sheet, but we quickly realized that this approach wouldn't scale to the hundreds of active projects we had going on.

We then started using the timer functionality inside of Monday.com, which is our project management platform. That worked at some level, but I felt like it was too granular and time con-suming for the team because it required tracking every task and there was no macro level roll up of the data. Before we removed that task-level tracking, we introduced a weekly time audit that was the perfect balance between micro-level detail and macro-level tracking.

This way, in 15 – 20 minutes, once a week, our team members were able to note what they had worked on in 15-minute incre-ments. As we started to roll this out, one of the developers on my team properly used The Circle of Life as he shared his feedback in a monthly self-review form that he submitted.

Here's what he said:

"I have one concern. This is regarding our redundant time track-ers. I think we have a lot of time trackers, and it is not effective anymore. We have Hubstaff, Monday.com, and weekly reports now. When a team member is in production mode, those track-ers will not be effective because I end up spending 30 mins or

more per day instead of working on projects. I think we should carefully study these time trackers because I think they are redundant and ineffective."

There are multiple reasons why I was so pleased with this feedback from my developer. First of all, he was concerned about how effective we were as a team. When we are effective as a team, we serve two valuable purposes. The first is that we can make the company more productive and profitable when we are efficient in how we work. The second reason that I deeply valued his feedback is because we don't ever intend to frustrate our team members. Frustrated team members don't do their best work. And that leads to the third and equally important reason. My developer was concerned about the triple tracking that I had unintentionally allowed because it would frustrate productivity and lead to not serving our clients at the highest level.

Because we've taught our team how to use The Circle of Life in their day-to-day decisions, this frees me and the other leaders on our team to focus on strategic objectives. Replicating yourself in your team is one of the major leverage points that entrepreneurs and leaders around the world need to master, and this simple framework can help you do just that.

Putting it into practice:

Think about what you would have done differently in your last business decision if you would have used The Circle of Life?

Write down your thoughts and put them in front of you for the next few weeks to remind you of this important mindset and decision-making tool.

And don't forget that in the book bonuses, I go deep on how and why we created our guiding principles. These guiding principles have helped us expand how we use The Circle of Life, and they are a massive part of the reason why our marketing firm has been able to skyrocket its growth over the past few years. Learn more about our guiding principles here: https://atomicwords.com/resources or just scan the QR code below:

CHAPTER 10

Engineered Conversations

"The most important thing is to keep the most important thing the most important thing."
— Donald P. Coduto

I remember it like it was yesterday. It was late at night, long after my entire team had gone home for the day. I had been sitting at my desk, making notes, doing research and diving into the analytics that my client had provided me. I was sitting there trying to figure out what the fastest path to success would be for them.

My client had paid me a small discovery fee up front of a few thousand dollars so that I could uncover what wasn't working in their marketing and how to correct it and turn their marketing into a consistently positive return on investment in their business. The challenge was that my client was currently working with one of his good friends. From what I understood, he had gone to high school together and grown their businesses side by side for a season. Now, granted, this friend of theirs had probably gotten them results up to a certain point, but in my estimation, the current marketing campaigns had stopped being effective after my client had reached the three-million-dollar-a-year mark. Now, my client was breaking eight million dollars a year in revenue, and his current challenge was that he was struggling to bring in enough work to keep his crews busy. My client was in the home services space, and in addition to wanting to keep his existing crews busy, he needed to break that elusive eight-figure mark and get to the big ten-million-dollar revenue level.

In an ideal world, I love to see my clients spend between 10 – 15% of their topline revenue on marketing. When they do that, they see consistent growth and often become the market leaders in their space. As I sat and looked at the current strategy my client was operating under, he was only spending about 1.5% of his revenue on marketing, and because of that was seeing incredibly low returns.

How was I going to be able to overcome multiple hurdles in the presentation I had to give the following day and also ensure that my team and I were serving my client at the highest level? There were multiple challenges that had to be overcome. The first was that I had to kindly but directly show my client that his existing marketing vendor was no longer helping him, and in all reality probably hurting his business. How do you tell someone that their friend has been causing them more harm than good? While I'm sure that his friend didn't set out to intentionally hurt my client, the data was clear. They were doing completely ineffective work, which was resulting in their paid and organic search traffic yielding no results, while also tanking their search rankings in Google.

The second challenge was that I had to inform my client that if he didn't at least step up to investing 5% of their revenue in marketing, then their competitors (no matter how large or small) would continue to nibble away at their market share and profits. There have been plenty of times when I've been brought in to consult with the goal of saving money. While I love doing that in many cases, there are equally as many situations where the best path is actually to increase the marketing investment so that revenue *and* profits increase steadily as well.

The last big challenge for the presentation was that the friend of my client had taken it upon himself to say some negative things about me. While I didn't take this personally because I knew the source of the negative comments, I did know that in order to serve my client well, I would have to positively confront these accusations. My estimation was that the existing vendor had bad-mouthed me because they were afraid that another client may leave them and come to work with my team. I rarely invest the time and resources to directly market against my competitors. The handful of clients that came to me from this "competitor" had done so without me soliciting them and had stated that they no longer felt like the competitor cared about them and their business.

So I had three big challenges to overcome, and what mattered most to me was that my client would get the support and results they deserved regardless of which vendor they ultimately decided to work with. Earlier in the book we talked about framing conversations effectively, and I've found that even before I begin writing a client proposal, or even before I begin speaking, it helps to set the intention of my heart. I make it a consistent practice to say to myself and also aloud to clients that, "It is my intention to serve you at the highest level, and give you the absolute best service and results that we can during our time together."

When I begin my interaction with those intentions, I feel confident that regardless of how long a season I get to spend with someone, that they will get the very best of me. As I sat there contemplating how I could best serve my client in this strategic blueprint that he had invested in, I decided to be strong and kind, and share my honest assessment. I knew that being kind and candid would truly serve my client at the highest level now and in the long run.

Because I had specific goals for the presentation that I had the next day, I took time to not only create a slide deck presentation as I commonly do, but I also took time to write out the outline of what I wanted to cover. As I reviewed my outline, I asked myself the following questions:

- How can I share my true intentions in the beginning of the meeting so that I can establish trust with my client?
- How can I display true care and service to my client while also directly addressing the huge deficiencies I see in their current marketing?

- How can I kindly and respectfully address the bad-mouthing that the current vendor had directed my way?
- How can I explain that the reason I recommend my client spend more is because it's truly in their best interest?

These were just a few of the questions I wrote down, and I chose to put them into "how" question format for a strategic reason. You see, I've learned over the years that when we pose "how" questions to our conscious and subconscious mind, the absolute best results come back to us. I believe that our minds tap into the power of the Universe when we do that, and this allows us to bring divine inspiration and results to our work.

Little by little, as I sat and contemplated the questions I'd written down for myself, the right words and the right structure came to me. I updated my presentation to reflect the new structure and I also updated my outline that I would be referring to as I shared my findings with my client the next day. Even though it ended up being a longer night of work than I often get to invest in, by the time I went to bed, I was very pleased with the plan I had created. I wasn't worried about the presentation the next day, as I knew that I had engineered the best possible conversation that would serve my client at the highest level.

At the end of this chapter I'll share with you exactly how the presentation turned out, and more importantly, I'll share with you how taking this approach led to amazing results for my client.

Now that I've shared one example of what engineering a conversation can look like, I'd like to share some of the specific elements that I use when I'm creating the framework for an engineered conversation. When you understand and master these tools, you'll be able to be incredibly strategic and successful in all your day-to-day conversations. And just as importantly, those crucial conversations that have the potential to make or break your business and your important personal relationships will be smoother and more effective.

I like to use something I call the BRIDGES model as I plan for an engineered conversation that I'm going to have. I believe that if I can build a BRIDGES during a crucial conversation, that this is the best path for me to serve my audience at the highest level.

BRIDGES stands for:

- Beginnings
- Results
- Intentions
- Direction (vision)
- Game Plan
- Explainers (stories)
- Summary

I realize that this acronym is not the shortest or easiest to remember, but I'd strongly encourage you to write it down, refer back to it, and memorize it over time. The conversations that we need to engineer in our lives are rarely simple and easy conversations, so it's worth taking time to plan out and engineer the entire conversation using the BRIDGES model.

Here's the short version of the BRIDGES model that I put into action with my client who I had to give the presentation to. Even though I've chosen to leave the identity of my client confidential, for the sake of this example, let's call my client Tom.

Here's how my conversation with him went during the presentation:

[Beginnings]

In the beginning or opening, I always start with appreciation and gratitude. While this seems simple, I'm shocked at how many times a new prospective vendor of mine doesn't open their presentations this way. I would strongly encourage you to NEVER begin a presentation without an opening of gratitude.

"Hi, Tom. Thank you for taking the time to meet with us today. I'm grateful for the opportunity to serve you and I appreciate you sharing all the information that you have so far."

[Results]

In this section I'm using an anchor so I can help Tom focus on what I know is his big goal is. He stated this to me in our initial meeting, and I know that I can serve him best by anchoring him back on the results he desires.

"I remember that you shared with my team and me that the result you wanted was to have your marketing drive better opportunities in the form of leads to your sales team. I also

remember that one of the other results you wanted was to be able to clearly see what areas of your marketing were working effectively, and which areas needed improvement or elimination. So with those goals in mind, we've prepared this strategic one-year plan for you."

[Intentions]

Stating my intentions at this point helped lower any pressure or anxiety that existed in the room and reminded my client of my true heart's intentions. Stating your intentions will almost always provide emotional security to your audience.

"My intention in our time here together today is to serve you and your team at the highest level. Regardless of which vendor you choose to work with long term, I'm committed to being honest with you and also giving you the best possible service and advice in this phase of our engagement together. We are looking forward to engaging in the next phase and helping you crush your marketing goals. However, if for some reason you decide to take this strategy and implement it all yourself or with your existing vendor, that is OK with me as well. All that matters to me is that I am able to provide value to you and help you win in the long run, Tom."

Not only did I mean every word of what I said, but I also created a safe place for Tom because after I said that, he knew that I wasn't going to use some inappropriate high-pressure sales tactics on him. He knew (because I truly meant every word of it) that all I wanted was for him to win in the long run. This took

Tom from being on the defensive to being in a state where he could objectively discuss many of the challenging things we uncovered. It also let him know that in that moment I was simply there to consult with him and protect him in any way I could.

One of our deepest desires as humans is to feel safe, and anytime we can provide that type of environment for our audience, we will be able to move so much faster. We can move faster when our audience feels safe because they will almost always communicate with us more freely and make decisions from a place of confidence and safety. While I do believe that there are a few times where fear can be used from a place of love to protect someone, those times are not very common. I would strongly encourage you to create a safe place for your audience whenever possible. In my experience, that is when the biggest transformations can occur.

[Direction]

When you clearly communicate the direction you want to go, then your vision can become your audience's vision as well. Too often as entrepreneurs and leaders, we assume that everyone around us can read our minds. While I know that's not actually true (the mind reading part) I still catch myself making assumptions periodically. I choose to continually remind myself that I need to set the direction for those around me, and I need to take full ownership of communicating my vision clearly.

"Based on our earlier discussions and the information you and your team provided us, Tom, it's clear that you need to gener-

ate at least 50 highly qualified leads per month. It's also been clearly communicated that you don't have enough visibility on your current lead flow. I agree that it's important to create a lead-tracking system that will allow you to identify your actual lead flow, and the opportunities created from those leads. What we've put together in this 12-month strategic marketing plan will not only address the lead-flow issues, but will also dramatically increase your brands reach and credibility. This is important because when your brand is strong in your marketplace, your sales team will have an easier time consistently closing higher-dollar projects. So let's dive into each area of the holistic mar-keting plan we created for you now..."

While I won't bore you with the entire marketing plan that we presented to Tom, I will tell you that he eagerly reviewed each aspect of the plan with me. Because of how I had engineered and set up the conversation with BRIDGES, he was fully present and very interested in what my team and I had prepared.

[Game Plan]

As I mentioned in the earlier paragraph, I proceeded to break down the entire plan for Tom. The game plan truly is the nuts and bolts of whatever you need to work through. Often your game plan may contain sensitive topics. In my case I had to respond to the vendor's bad-mouthing of me. I also had to address the fact that his existing vendor was actually hurting his SEO. Because I had clearly stated my intentions, it was much easier to address these areas of concern. I was also care-ful to maintain a calm and kind tone of voice when addressing those items so that Tom was able to truly feel the sincerity of my heart as I addressed the concerning points.

As you get into the Game Plan phase of your engineered conversation, be direct and candid about all the nuts and bolts of what's going on. Also remember that how you make your audience feel as you address the heart of the matter will stick with them as much as the specifics of what you say.

As I mentioned, the Game Plan in Tom's case isn't relevant to share here in detail, but I hope that you understand that this is often the meat of the conversation. It's always wise to plan this part of your conversation in detail, as well, because delivery matters as much as content.

[Explainers]

While I wish that every single time we presented a large technical or marketing project our clients instantly understood every aspect of the plan, that is rarely, if ever, the case. Explainers are the stories that we use to convey complex or unfamiliar concepts to our audience. What I've learned over the years is that having a list of explainers handy (or as they are called in the Bible, "parables") will serve you well.

While my list of explainers is not comprehensive or complete yet, I used one of them earlier in the book when I explained SEO. Using that example of going to a conference and networking before you get on stage has been a clear and effective explainer for many years now.

148

I used that same explainer in my presentation meeting with Tom, and he instantly understood. Here's another example of an explainer I used with Tom when we were discussing the importance of consistent organic social media posting:

"I know that it's often hard to initially see or measure the value of posting on your social media channels, so let me explain it in a different way. If you think about the last time you traveled down our local Route 90 highway, at some point you probably saw a Geico billboard with their famous gecko. Now imagine that you took that route to work every day and saw the same billboard for a month or two. Then, one day, as you got onto the highway, you saw a new billboard advertisement from Geico. They caught your eye because the message and graphics were new and different compared to the last one. Now fast forward a few months and imagine yourself walking to your mailbox to get the mail. You open up your mail and see a letter from your existing insurance company. The notice they sent states that they will be increasing your auto insurance rate by 38%! In that moment, who do you think you're going to call to get a rate quote? The marketing statistics show that you'll call Geico.

The reasoning behind that is simple. Geico invested in locations where they could get repetitive impressions in front of you with their sign. Now, obviously, Geico may have been using other advertising channels on you too, but the point is this: When you are consistent in posting on social media, you begin to "buy" mental real estate in your prospect's mind. Then, when they hit a pain point in their life or business, you have brand presence, and they are much more likely to call you than a competitor who doesn't invest in consistent branding. Make sense?"

That is one of the explainers that I use to help people have a clear picture of how consistent organic social media posting works. I also use that explainer to set a clear expectation. Organic posting is not the same as paid traffic, but in the long haul, it can have similar branding results, which, in turn, can become a huge booster to your sales activities.

Now take a moment and think about your own products and services. Think about the objectives that you need to achieve as entrepreneur and leader. What explainers can you develop that will help you convey the message that best serves your audience? Take a moment to jot some ideas down now, and then flesh them out later on.

If you're stuck (as I am sometimes) and can't think of any good explainers in the moment, that's OK. Use the power of your subconscious mind and simply write down and ask yourself, *"What would be the best explainer for this complex topic?"* And then get ready. Odds are, if you're like me, the ideas will come when you're in the shower, or driving, or on a walk. Jot the ideas down when they come to you, and then flesh them out fully later.

[Summary]

Now that you've engineered your conversation by using the Beginnings, talked about the Results you want, shared your

Intentions, clearly laid out the Direction and vision you have, and used colorful and easy-to-understand Explainers, it's time to bring it all home with a Summary.

When we summarize things, we can reinforce what was covered by using the power of repetition. When you're able to pre-plan your BRIDGES, you can make notes for yourself on which key points should be in the summary. If you're free-flowing during the BRIDGES conversation, then jotting down a few key notes as you present will help you summarize the conversation.

Ideally, I like to call out agreements and action items that were determined during the conversation. This way you can send a follow-up note after your conversation to reinforce, once again, what was covered. Repetition is such a key factor in effective communication, so don't ever be afraid to use it.

The last point I'll make about the BRIDGES framework is that during the entire process, you should allow time to pause and listen to any feedback or questions that your audience has. Communication is only effective when it's two ways, and so as much as you prepare to deliver clear and impactful messaging through your BRIDGES, I'd strongly recommend that you allow spaces to ask questions and listen carefully. Being an active listener is one of the simplest ways to build trust and ensure that both you and your audience (an audience of one or many) is being served by your message.

Rehearsing a Crucial Conversation Is Often Wise

When I first started rehearsing conversations aloud or in my own head, I felt silly. But the end result of rehearsing was that I was able to deliver truly impactful communication. In order to serve your audience at the highest level, I believe it's wise to consider all the different avenues that the conversation may go. If you pre-plan for any concerns, frustrations, or out-of-left-field questions that may come up, then you'll be able to respond instead of react. Reactionary communication almost always ends up in miscommunication and hurt feelings. Responsive communication is what a master communicator does to guide the conversation and serve the audience.

One great way to improve how you engineer future conversations is to reflect on a recent crucial conversation that didn't go as well as you had hoped it would. Making note of the points in the conversation that ended up being turning points is a good first step. Once you do that, think about how you could have calmly responded to continue to guide the conversation in a positive direction.

It takes practice and intention to master in-conversation awareness, but the end result is worth it. Before I sat down today to complete this part of the chapter, I was having a conversation with my partner, Rachel. We were talking about one of our friends who is going through a challenging time in their life. As Rachel shared her feelings about the situation, I noticed that I was having a feeling in my chest of slight anxiety. While I continued to actively listen to Rachel share her thoughts,

I continued to be aware of my own feelings, and I realized that for some reason I felt the need to "teach" Rachel about the situation. As I identified that feeling, I realized that it was coming from a place of insecurity or pride. My reactionary feeling of needing to teach Rachel something was the opposite of what Rachel actually needed. In that moment, Rachel needed me to be an active listener. She needed me to validate her feelings and hold space for her and the journey she was on.

I have failed to respond in an effective manner many times over the years, but the more that I set a positive intention in my heart when a conversation begins, the more I'm able to truly serve those around me that I'm communicating with. Crucial conversations happen every day in our lives, and I believe that it's our job as the entrepreneurs and leaders in this world to continue to develop our self-awareness. Continued cultivation of self-awareness has, in my experience, helped me to develop more situational awareness and emotional intelligence. We've all heard it a thousand times, but the saying, "People don't remember what you said, they remember how you made them feel" is absolutely true. I also believe that people will remember what we said much more readily when we first ensure that we have created a space where they feel heard and understood.

Listening with a Heart of Service

Much of this book has been written about the tools and frameworks that I use on a daily basis to prepare and deliver what I have to share with my audience. I also believe that it's equally important to continually develop our observational skills and our listening skills. Listening intently to what others are saying, taking time to contemplate what else they may be trying to communicate (essentially reading between the lines), and truly setting your heart's intention on serving them at the highest level is a great place to start.

One of the things that I've learned over the years and that I regularly share with my team is that when someone is frustrated and upset, we actually deliver at least half of the relief they are seeking by simply hearing them out. Truly listening with empathy and compassion to someone's frustrations and concerns resolves so many customer service issues, and yet it is very easy for us to become defensive. I'm very grateful for the fact that one of the amazing people on my leadership team, Danielle Ortiz, is incredibly skilled at listening to a client's frustration without taking it personally. Recently, Danielle came on our company's podcast, *BME Stories,* and shared how she chooses to not take things personally, and instead just looks for positive solutions when she has the opportunity to serve a client that is upset about something.

Personally, I've started to realize that when I feel the need to react to what someone is saying and defend myself, or even defend my team or someone else that is being complained about, those feelings come from a place of insecurity. Overall I wouldn't say that I struggle with insecurity in my life and in the roles I fulfill, but in those moments when I do feel the reactionary side of me coming to the surface, it gives me an opportunity to become more self-aware and evaluate what is causing the root of that insecurity. One thing that has made a massive difference in this area is that I've integrated meditation into my daily life for many years now. The practice of mindfulness allows me to pause before reacting. There are spaces between the moments where we can choose how we respond. At first that concept may sound crazy, but I'm confident that if you implement mindfulness and meditation into your daily practice, you too will start to recognize those spaces between the moments where you get to decide if you're going to react or respond.

As you move forward in the coming days and weeks, I encourage you to ask yourself, "How can I slow down and choose my responses, even when I'm feeling stressed or emotional?" If you simply ask that question of yourself, and are open to receiving the real answers that your subconscious mind and spirit bring back to you, I believe that you'll be able to make massive improvements in this area of your life.

The more we slow down and choose our responses, and the more we practice mindfulness and intentional communication, the fewer regrets we'll have and the more we'll be able to serve those around us at the highest level. Be patient with yourself and focus on making incremental improvements over time. If you do this, you and those around you will start to see the change in who you are and how you operate.

Put it into practice:

Take a few minutes to write down a list of a few crucial conversations that you've had recently and then ask yourself:

Where were the crucial turning points in that conversation?

How could I have planned for something like that ahead of time?

What could I do to respond in the moment in a positive way?

How can I become an active listener that truly serves those around me by holding space for them?

If you've struggled with planning and engineering your conversations effectively in the past, that's OK! So have I. But instead of continuing to struggle, you can download a copy of the BRIDGES worksheet at https://atomicwords.com/resources or just scan the QR code below:

CHAPTER 11

Dueling Words

"Only one who devotes himself to a cause with his whole strength and soul can be a true master. For this reason mastery demands all of a person."
— Albert Einstein

I remember it like it was yesterday.

I was sitting in my friend Tim's office and I was telling him about how bad I felt about everything that had happened. My first business, where I did construction and remodeling, had failed during the housing market crash of 2007 – 2008. I had gotten separated from my first wife and was in the midst of getting a divorce. My childhood best friend had just died at the very young age of 26 from complications related to spina bifida, and I was nearly broke.

As many of us do in situations of pain, I was wallowing in my misery and complaining about my life. I said to Tim, "I suck at business, and I failed."

Tim said to me, *"That's wrong, Gabe. If you keep talking like that, you're just going to hurt yourself. You've got to stop using language like that if you want to get through this. You are going through a painful time like many other contractors are right now, but blaming yourself for what happened isn't productive, and you've got to stop it right now."*

In that moment, my chest started hurting, and I really didn't like what Tim had to say to me. But, I knew he was right. And even though Tim and I are no longer in contact, I'm grateful to him for that moment when he called me on my bullshit and told me to stop speaking in a negative and unproductive way. That was one of the first times that a friend of mine challenged my language choices and patterns, and it helped me start the journey of self-evaluation as it relates to the words that I use.

Fast forward to ten years after that conversation. By this point I had processed through and resolved many of the wounds I got from my childhood and from the hellacious loss of my first large business. But, I was still repeating some of the ineffective behaviors as they related to my self-talk. I was also not communicating as effectively as I would soon be able to after discovering and adopting the tools and frameworks I've shared with you in this book so far.

One day in 2018, shortly after I had met my friend Jay Crouch and we had started working together, I was explaining something to him, and he stopped me. He said, *"Gabe, you're smashing things together and convoluting them. When you do this, you're creating confusion instead of clarity. Let's break this down component by component first."*

That was the start of a very productive and useful ongoing dialogue that Jay and I had over the coming months. He would regularly challenge what I had to say, and he would help me become clearer in my thoughts and in what I had to communicate. I've met plenty of people who claim to be communication experts, but Jay was actually a master at it. And he didn't claim to be an expert in communication. He was just incredibly focused and intentional when it came to how and when he communicated with me and with others. It probably stems from his engineering mind and from his incredible experience in the technology and startup industries. But, regardless of where he picked it up, he is someone that I will always be grateful for because he chose to serve me in incredible ways during the time that we got to work together.

Leveling up your communication skills

I do not believe that we grow and change in a vacuum. I believe that as entrepreneurs and leaders it's our responsibility to engineer environments and support systems that will allow us to grow rapidly in the areas where we need development. Because of this belief that I have, I regularly complete the following exercises to evaluate myself and where I'm headed.

One of the first exercises that I do, which was first introduced to me by my time management coach and friend Lisa Crilley

Mallis, is completing a time study. At first, I hated doing this, and even today when I do them, they are not the most fun thing in the world, but I've come to appreciate their effectiveness. A time study is simply the process of writing down what you've done every 15 minutes throughout the day. My friend Alex Charfen teaches this to his community as well, and he recommends not only completing the time study for your working hours but also tracking the rest of your day as well.

When I first did a time study, I was shocked at how much time I wasted doing meaningless things like checking email (but not responding to it) or browsing social media or YouTube. I typically do a time study for two weeks, and then I sit down and evaluate the patterns that I see. When I sat down to evaluate things, I was surprised to see how much ineffective communication was going on. I had purposeless meetings without agendas, and because I wasn't making clear asks using ARC or frames like "The problem I'm trying to solve…", there was a ton of back-and-forth communication that wasn't resolving in clarity as fast as it could have. I also realized that I wasn't creating the environment around me that would challenge my communication skills and help me grow.

Once I realized this, I had a choice. I could ignore my findings, or I could make choices to change things. I chose to change things, and that led me into the second exercise that I now regularly complete on a quarterly or even monthly basis. That exercise is the exercise of reviewing my calendar and eliminating things that no longer serve me, while adding in time blocks and appointments that will allow me to move towards my goals. In seasons where I realize that I've been slipping in my communication development, I choose to spend time with those who will challenge me and help me grow in this area.

Sometimes those people are friends and family members who debate with me in a healthy and productive manner. Other times I choose to hire consultants and coaches who specialize in leadership development, communication, and team culture development. While I get benefits from both scenarios, I often get the most benefit from those I pay to guide and support me. There are a few reasons for this, and I believe that they are worth explaining so that you can be intentional about how you engineer support for yourself in your entrepreneurial journey.

First off, I believe that it is very important to pay for coaching and mentorship. The reason for this is that when we get free advice, we are less likely to implement it; but when we've paid for advice, we take it more seriously and are more likely to implement it. I've often told my coaches that the reason I'm paying them for the time is so that I show up for myself and do the work that I know I need to do. Even as a business coach myself, I tell my coaching clients the same thing. A huge part of why my coaching time with them is effective is because they are choosing to pay to spend time on themselves with my support and guidance. My coaching is by invitation or application only, and I'm definitely not the coach for everyone out there because I'm pretty direct about the advice I give. But, regardless of who you choose to hire as a coach, I do have some advice that has served me well on that front.

Secondly, I get maximum value from the coaching sessions I pay for with my coaches when I show up to the sessions with a clear understanding of what I want to accomplish. I will often write an outline of what I want to accomplish during the season that I am going to be coached by them, and then for each call I either have a preset agenda, or I send an agenda before the call so my coach can be prepared to support me. My coaching clients almost always come to our calls with a clear agenda of what they want to achieve, which I really appreciate. On the other side of things, I'm shocked to see so many people who are not proactive in this manner, and simply ask or let their coach dictate their direction and focus. In my experience and opinion, this is not an effective way to level up in any area of your life.

When we take full ownership of the growth we want to see in ourselves is when we actually get the results we want and need. That is why I continue to bring people into my life who are willing to help me challenge how I communicate, and what I think about as an entrepreneur and leader. Our ability to communicate effectively is one of the biggest leverage points we have, and so I would encourage you to find and hire people to give you SPARC (Specific Praise and Really Specific Candor) about your communication.

Putting it into practice:

Before you move on to the next chapter, send a clear ARC to five people in your life who you trust will be kind, respectful, and direct in their responses. You can use this format exactly, or modify it to match your needs, but be sure to use ARC. Here's a template of what you can send to them:

Hi [First name],

I'd like to **Ask** for your feedback on how I communicate.

The **Reason** I need your help is because I value your opinion and I need some outside perspective on my communication skills. You are one of five close friends and family members that I've asked for feedback, so I'd really appreciate anything you can share with me.

The **Context** is that I'm reading a book called *Atomic Words* and there is a challenge in the book to get feedback on my communication skills.

So I want to know:

1. Where am I strongest in my communication?

2. Where can I improve my communication skills?

3. Is there anything else that you can share with me that will help me become a more effective communicator?

Thank you for taking the time to give me your honest feedback. I appreciate you.

[Your name]

You may have to follow up a few times in order to get responses, and that's OK. Follow up and get their feedback. Regardless of what feedback they share with you, thank them for their time and investment in you when they send it back.

Once you've gathered the feedback from those you asked, take time to evaluate what they shared. Remember that some feedback may be inaccurate or ineffective, and that's OK. Don't take it personally. What I do suggest is that you carefully consider what is said and consider the following questions:

1. Does this feedback feel accurate, and what does it bring up in my heart and mind as I consider it?

2. Do I notice any patterns in the feedback that I received?

3. What positive feedback did I receive that shows me my strengths that I can maximize even more?

4. What critical feedback did I receive that I can use in a positive way to grow in my communication skills?

5. Lastly, who in my life can I pay to coach and challenge me as it relates to my communication skills, habits, and behaviors?

Taking time to gather feedback, evaluate it, and implement the beneficial suggestions that we receive is a highly effective way to grow our communication skills. I would encourage you to complete this exercise once or twice a year, as this will help you continually grow in this critical area of your life. Entrepreneurs and leaders who continually level up their communication skills reach their entrepreneurial goals much faster.

If you'd like to get a copy of the worksheet that you can use for self-evaluation of your own communication, or to use with a partner, then check out that section in the book bonuses here: https://atomicwords.com/resources or just scan the QR code below:

CHAPTER 12

Communication Wizards

"A wizard is never late, nor is he early, he arrives precisely when he means to." (Gandalf)
—J. R. R. Tolkien

Recently, my son began reading *The Hobbit* and *The Lord of The Rings* series, and so as he's been reading, we've been watching the movies that came out over the past couple of decades. One of the patterns I've noticed in the movies is that the wizard, Gandalf, always shows up at just the right time and ends up saving the day. The rest of the cast in the movies have to slog through some pretty unappealing situations. Ultimately, though, this is what develops their stamina and character and helps them become the men, hobbits, elves, and dwarves that they were meant to be.

In my opinion, that is how life works as it relates to becoming a communication wizard. We often begin our journey making many different mistakes, and at first it seems like no one will ever understand us. It's discouraging and difficult to get any kind of positive results when we sit down to write, or when we have a sales conversation, or when we try to coach our teams toward success. This is part of the journey that we must embark on in order to truly master communication at the wizardly level.

There have been many times where I made massive mistakes, hurt people's feelings, and equally as bad, communicated things that ended up costing people a lot of time and money they didn't necessarily have to waste in the first place. The journey to become a communication wizard often has its trials and its disappointments, but don't let that discourage you. In the midst of what may seem like a really messy and discouraging time, I know that there are things you can learn and things you can be grateful for.

Some of my all-time favorite movie lines come from Gandalf and Frodo as well:

"I wish it need not have happened in my time," said Frodo.

"So do I," said Gandalf, "and so do all who live to see such times. But that is not for them to decide. All we have to decide is what to do with the time that is given us."
—J.R.R. Tolkien, *The Fellowship of the Ring*

That last line always stands out to me. *"All we have to decide is what to do with the time that is given us."* That is something I think about frequently, and when I do ponder that statement, it reminds me that regardless of where I am at in my journey of communication skill improvement, I can always do the best that I can in the moment that I'm in. Granted, in only a matter of weeks or months, I will probably have gained more communication skills, tools, and frameworks that will make me more effective. But in this moment, I can use what I do have and what I do know.

I've also learned that when I reflect back on previous situations and evaluate how I communicated, it's ideal to do just that: evaluate. Judging our past selves is futile because we only knew what we knew then. It's easy to fall into the pattern of judging our past selves using the knowledge and experience we have today, but in doing that we don't complete The Wisdom Triangle. If we carefully evaluate ourselves without judgment, that will often lead to the wisdom and realization that our past self did the best that we could with the experience, information, and resources we had at the time. So please, don't be too hard on yourself. Take this journey one step at a time, and you'll grow and progress and find new levels of wisdom over time.

Playing chess in your conversations

One of my favorite games to play is Chess. I don't really enjoy many other board games, card games, or video games of any kind, but chess continues to be an all-time favorite year after year for me. One of the reasons that I love playing chess is that there are no two games that are exactly alike. According to Jonathan Schaeffer, a computer scientist from the University of Alberta, *"The possible number of chess games is so huge that no one will invest the effort to calculate the exact number."*

And that is probably why I love playing chess so much. I will never sit at the same board twice, and I will never face the exact same strategy from my opponent even if I play the same person over and over.

The game starts out in a familiar and orderly manner, but after both players make their first move, there are instantly 400 possible board configurations after that. After the players each move a second time, 197,742 possible board configurations. And after three moves, there are 121 million possible board configurations. Beyond the third move by both players, the number of possible board configurations and outcomes becomes nearly infinite.

Our conversations are similar. They often start in familiar ways and with familiar patterns, but they rarely follow the exact same path as any previous conversation that we have had.

In my opinion, what is equally as fascinating as the likely infinite possibilities of a chess game is the fact that people can, in real time, analyze their competitor's moves, thwart them, and end up ultimately winning the game by checkmate. How this is possible is a testament to the amazing qualities that our minds possess. Observing that complex of a game, and finding a way to win it, is something that will forever amaze me. The game of chess is estimated to be 1,500 years old at this point, and while I'm not a grandmaster in chess, or even close to that, it is a game that I continue to improve on while simultaneously learning many communication and business lessons from playing it.

When I play chess, I study what potential moves my opponent is going to make, and then I make counter moves to defend against their attacks. I continually look to identify ways to achieve my objective of getting a checkmate on my opponent's king as well. Or sometimes, if I can quickly destroy their position, they forfeit, and I win.

When I first realized the connection between chess and effective communication, it immediately helped me have more productive and impactful conversations. Instead of thinking that I needed to "beat" my opponent in a conversation, I reframed the conversation as a positive game. In this chess game in my mind, I sit third party, essentially envisioning myself hovering above myself and whoever I'm speaking to. In sitting third party to the conversation I get to evaluate what is being said and observe what reactions each person has (including my own reactions). I also translate the goal in this positive mental chess match into something that will ultimately be a win win win for everyone involved.

The "checkmate" that I'm going for is to have my audience (of one or multiple people) achieve a positive outcome in their life. By simultaneously being in the conversation, while also observing the conversation from a third-party perspective, I am able to temper my responses, plan my future statements and points, and carefully guide my audience to the positive destination that is mutually beneficial for me, for them, and for all of those that will be impacted by our conversation.

And that leads me to another point: communication between two parties is virtually impossible to keep siloed to those two people. As social animals, we inevitably share our conversations with other people. Sometimes this happens once, and sometimes, like in the case of this book, conversations I've had with my friends will be repeated hundreds of thousands of times by those who read this book.

What's important to remember is that our conversations are never in a vacuum. They ultimately spill over to many other people in our own lives and in the lives of our audience. This is why playing "chess" during our conversations is often beneficial. Sitting third party to a conversation allows me to:

- Prepare my opening comments.
- Monitor how they are received.
- Adjust my approach and follow-up thoughts.
- And ultimately serve the audience at the highest level by skillfully guiding them to the win, which is ultimately a win for both of us and all those that we'll interact with in the future.

I believe that we have more impactful conversations in a day than we realize. I've started to fully appreciate this fact more recently. I first noticed at a deeper level what the impact of my words was when one of my team members started quoting things I said during our end-of-day office routine. Since we are a worldwide team of experts, we use Google Chat as one of our primary community building and communication tools, and so at the end of the day, Joyce posts a quote and photo and reminds everyone to close up their tasks for the day and also prepare for the coming day ahead.

She's been doing this for a long time for our team, so when she started putting things I said to the team in the morning huddle on these graphics, I was surprised and happy to see them. One of the first ones she posted said this:

"We believe that radical candor will help us continually grow and confront things in a positive manner." — Gabe Arnold, CEO

When I saw that, my honest and first reaction was *"Did I say that?"* The recording of our daily huddle proved that I did.

The next day, Joyce posted another thing that I said:

"I truly believe that most people are acting from good intentions deep down, and when you view the world this way, it quickly becomes beautiful and peaceful." — Gabe Arnold, CEO

I was proud of that one. I didn't really intend it to be a quotable statement, but now it's something I use periodically in my social media posts and elsewhere. The reason I'm sharing this with you is because each and every one of us says powerful and impactful things to those around us on a daily basis. Instead of letting those moments of great impact be by happenstance, I believe that it is our job as entrepreneurs and leaders to be intentional about saying things that matter.

We can win the game of conversational chess by planning ahead, observing where our audience is at in the moment, and setting a clear intention of winning the conversation in a way that leaves both ourselves and our audiences in a much more positive place. I intentionally put this chapter towards the end of the book because this skill of sitting third party and playing conversational chess is something that takes time and patience to learn. Even though I've been actively taking this approach for well over a decade now, I still feel like I have an immense amount to learn about skillfully guiding conversations in this manner.

My journey to having any level of skill in this area began by simply reflecting on and evaluating the conversations that I had in the recent days and weeks before I sat down to think. I would ask myself:

- Did I begin the conversation with clear intentions and with a clear outcome that would create a win win win for us and those we influence?
- Did we accomplish something positive in that conversation that helped us both move forward, or at least helped my audience to move forward?
- Was I consciously aware of how my audience was feeling as we communicated?
- Was I consciously aware of how I was feeling during that conversation?
- What were the turning points in the conversation that went well?

- What were the turning points in the conversation that were negative or ineffective as it related to the outcome I wanted to achieve?
- Where could I have been a more active listener during the conversation?
- Where could I have shown more empathy and compassion?
- What else did I learn during that conversation?

By meditating on those questions, and often journaling about my responses to the questions, I began creating an awareness of what I was doing when I was in a conversation. And piece by piece, I started implementing a more proactive approach that allowed me to guide the conversational chess game in real time.

The first step for me, which we've already discussed earlier in this book, was to set a clear, and almost always stated aloud, intention for the conversation. That immediately set the tone for what we would talk about, and it also helped me stay focused on the outcome that I wanted to achieve. I'm not completely sure why it has this effect, but when I state aloud something like *"my intention in our time together today is to serve you at the highest level and help us both clarify what the next steps are in this project,"* it immediately slows time down for me and allows me to enter a state where I'm actively listening and observing. This level of engagement in the conversation helps me to provide thoughtful and intentional responses. It helps me limit, or even in some cases eliminate, reactionary thoughts and statements that stall out or derail free-flowing and open communication.

After getting clear about my intentions, I started to pay closer attention to how I was feeling in the moment and how my audience was feeling. Were they leaning in towards me? Were their arms crossed? Did they move away from me (physically, or even in a virtual setting on a video call)? Where were their eyes focused? Did it look like they were comfortable, or was the topic matter stirring up emotions that caused them to either change their tone, or start to get teary eyed, or cry?

As I started to observe the physical communication that my audience was giving back to me, it helped me become aware of what I was communicating physically. The same was true for my observation and awareness of their emotional state. The more I paid attention to their emotions, the more I started to honor my own emotions in the situation.

And while prior to this part of the book, we haven't even scratched the surface of body language, there are a few things that I'll say about that here so you can begin your journey in studying and understanding that part of the communication that you have with others. One book that helped me understand body language at a deeper level was from Joe Navarro titled *What Every Body is Saying*.

That book helped me become even more aware of what other people were saying to me with their bodies, and it helped refine and clarify some of the things that I have picked up organically over the years. This is an area that I continue to obsessively observe and study, but this book is not meant to be the ultimate source or authority on this topic. With that being said, I will share some of the primary body language and tonal nuances that will help get you started in the right direction on this front.

Body language to observe and mimic

One of the first motivators that drove me to study body language at a deeper level was the realization that when we mimic the behaviors and body language of our audience (an audience of one or many), they will immediately and instinctively begin to trust us more. As I mentioned in the beginning of this book, all of the things I'm sharing here with you must be used for good. This is one of the things that when used in a manipulative manner is not only incredibly hurtful to others but is even more damaging to your long-term success. So please, please use this wisely.

From my research and experience, mimicking the body language of others stimulates the primal need to belong. In herds of animals, they will often reject one of the group who doesn't look like them. This is for the protection of the entire herd and so the individuals in the herd know that they need to fall in line, act like, and look like the rest of the herd. While that statement probably makes you physically uncomfortable as an entrepreneur and leader (because we are generally individualists), it's a real factor of life and communication that we need to understand in order to serve our audiences well.

Mimicking the body language and behavior of others to a relatively close degree is not only important from a trust standpoint but it also (in my personal experience) creates deeper connections that can be felt both intellectually and emotionally. Because my goal is always to connect more deeply with the goal of serving at the highest level, these are things that I regularly do:

- If the person I'm speaking to is leaning back in their chair and relaxing, I do the same.
- If they are leaning into the conversation and physically moving a little closer, I move in too.
- If they cross their arms, I cross my arms.
- If they cross their legs, or push their chair back from the table or desk, I do the same thing.
- If they are speaking more rapidly than I normally do, I speed up the meter of my speech.
- If they are using an excited tone, I get excited too.
- If they are mellow and very matter of fact in their tone and words, I match their speech with a similar approach.
- When I intentionally want to have a closer and more intimate conversation, I move in physically closer. The reason for this is that our nervous system dictates how we feel as much as our mind does. If we let someone in closer physically, our brain essentially has no choice but to say to itself, *"Well, I must trust this person because I'm allowing them to be so close to me."*
- When someone uses specific phraseology, or cusses in conversation, I will speak in similar ways while, of course, also living up to my own personal standards and ethics.

- If someone stands directly face to face to address me, I move into that slightly closer so they know I'm comfortable engaging them that way.
- If I notice that they prefer talking to people while standing side by side with them, I model that behavior and allow them to stand in a way that makes them comfortable.
- If they are intense with their eye contact, so am I.
- And if they are more comfortable looking away frequently, then I will look away as well, and simply match their eye patterns.
- And last but not least, my friend Chris taught me recently that when I choose to match the breathing patterns of those I'm communicating with, that can create a deep soul connection and much more rapid safety and trust in the conversation. So that is something new and fun I am working on.

As I mentioned, this is an area that I constantly study and I continually learn more about. The book I mentioned above is a great resource that will allow you to learn even more about body language, and even before you read it, I encourage you to just start being more intentional about observing how people are physically behaving while they are in communication with you.

There are a lifetime of secrets and wisdom in the bodies that we have and in the bodies of others we are communicating with. When we are clear in our genuine and loving intentions, and we truly begin to observe our conversations sitting third party, amazing communication and healing can occur on both sides. I hope that in the little bit of time we've spent in the book exploring body language, you've been inspired to go deeper on this front. I know for me, it is something that I continually study and enjoy learning more about.

Putting it into practice:

In order to become a communication wizard, it is important to master sitting third party to your conversations so that you can strategically guide them in real time.

What is the first thing you can do to become more aware and intentional in your conversations?

Body language is one of the loudest and most informative parts of a conversation.

What body language are you displaying in your conversations that supports the communication and connection you are intending to have?

What body language are you displaying that is detracting from your communication?

What body language can you start to observe in others so that you can provide them safety and a positive and trusting space to communicate in?

Last but not least, who in your life can you ask to practice applying the things you've learned in this book, *Atomic Words*?

In my experience getting a communication buddy is incredibly helpful as we learn these new skills.

One last amazing resource that I've put in the bonuses for this book is a conversation I had with a friend of mine about the power of mimicking and being aware of body language. You can check it out in the bonus section here: https://atomicwords.com/resources or just scan the QR code below:

Conclusion

Thank you so much for taking the time to read this book. While the journey of creating and publishing this book took some unexpected turns and took longer than I originally anticipated, I can say that from the first day I started drafting it almost two years before it ultimately was published, my goal has always been to empower entrepreneurs and leaders with impactful and effective communication tools.

The reason for this is that I believe that our impact as entrepreneurs and leaders is directly equivalent to our ability to communicate effectively. I know when I was starting out, I said stupid and hurtful things, communicated my ideas ineffectively, and was often left with a lot of frustration and hurt in my head and my heart.

Entrepreneurship (which by my definition is servant leadership) has plenty of challenges on its own, without adding in the fact that we are typically a very misunderstood group of people. In my experience, the misunderstanding is just as often caused by our own immature and underdeveloped communication habits as it is other people simply choosing not to try to understand our very different brains. If this book helps even one entrepreneur communicate their ideas more effectively so that they can make a positive impact on the world, then I've done my job correctly.

I also want to congratulate you and tell you how proud I am of you for finishing the book. While I don't believe all books should be completed, I do know that sticking with something, and learning and applying new skills. is what ultimately helps us grow up as entrepreneurs and leaders.

I realize that not every part of this book may be applicable to you. What I do ask is that you set a clear intention of what you plan to implement from what you learned here. Write down that intention, paste it in a calendar appointment for yourself, and set the date for three months from today. Or schedule an email to yourself with your intention for three months from now.

When you see that calendar note or email come back to you, see how you're progressing with your intentions as they relate to your improved communication. Once you evaluate your growth, I'd encourage you to repeat this exercise again.

Keep setting targets for yourself that are three months away, and watch how you grow and progress as an impactful and effective communicator.

Improving our communication skills is a lifelong process, but we do get to reap the rewards of our growth every time we make positive improvements. So keep at it, and remember that your words are Atomic Words. They are the words that bring ideas to life. They are the words that help others see themselves in a different light. They are the words that can ultimately leave a massive and positive impact on the world around you.

So choose your words wisely, and become a master of Atomic Words.

Speaking and Other Opportunities:

If you're interested in having me speak to your group, provide coaching or consulting, or having our team at Business Marketing Engine help you make your marketing as effective and impactful as you know it can be, please shoot me an email at hello@atomicwords.com, and my team and I will get back to you.

If you have any other questions or feedback on the book, I would love to hear from you on that as well, so use the same email, hello@atomicwords.com, to contact me.